REVELATION UNLOCKED

A PERSONAL COMMENTARY ON THE APOCALYPSE

BY

MICHAEL JARVIS

The Covenant Publishing Company Limited
121, Low Etherley, Bishop Auckland, Co. Durham, DL14 0HA

2009

First Edition 2009

ISBN 978-085205-076-7

Front cover: The keys pictured on the front cover are the actual keys to the city of Jerusalem, the same that were presented to General Allenby at the relief of Jerusalem in 1917. (See p. 75.) The author has seen and handled these keys, that are in the care of The Royal West Kent Regimental Museum, St Faith Street, Maidstone, Kent.

Published and printed by

The Covenant Publishing Company Limited
121, Low Etherley, Bishop Auckland, Co. Durham. DL14 0HA
United Kingdom

www.covpub.co.uk

REVELATION – Unlocked

Introduction

Is there a better place to start than with the Lord Jesus Himself?

Revelation is a much neglected and misunderstood part of the Bible. Many, if they think about it at all, consider it to be beyond their understanding, and give up on it before really trying to get to grips with it. Mostly our churches avoid it except for verses that are traditionally used at funerals: it would be better to teach it to the living, than wait until they are dead! Taking a quick look at its first and last few paragraphs, as one might with any other book, will show that it has an important message to give us.

This Book declares itself to be a prophecy, that is to say, it both 'forth tells' God's Word, and also foretells for our guidance, of things that are going to occur after it was recorded for us. It proclaims its author to be none other than the Risen Lord Jesus.

It is a vision or series of visions, of things to happen in the context of God's love, justice, judgement, mercy and of course His saving grace. Much of this is written in a sort of code, where identities and events are represented in symbolic forms, so that unless the meaning of the symbols is understood, the message is obscure.

Many are the ingenious codes that have been devised to conceal business or military messages from all except those for whom they are intended. This code is devised by God for the same reason. The gospel of salvation is openly expressed in simple and straightforward terms, and is intended to bring the ungodly to repentance and knowledge of Christ. By contrast, *Revelation* is constructed to be understood only by the faithful throughout the Christian period, who will diligently search the scriptures for the trail of clues or keys to unlock its message, and reveal the mind and purpose and programme of God for their own day. In doing this the destiny and identity of the 'Lost Sheep' to whom Jesus said he was sent becomes known, and where they may be found and what they have been doing, sometimes unwittingly, in His service through 2000 years, also becomes known.

Jesus uses some of the symbolic terms from His parables of the Kingdom, recorded in the Gospels, and also terminology from the Old Testament prophets. Christians who consider the O.T. to be 'old hat' and no longer of importance, bar themselves from ever making sense of *Revelation*, the special message from their professed Saviour and Lord.

When Jesus used parables He was continuing the tradition of the O.T. prophets, for example *Ezekiel* 37, visions of the dry bones, and two sticks, that show the intended destinies of Israel and Judah at some then future point in their histories. *Revelation*, starting with the then present and immediate future (about AD 90, when *Revelation* is believed to have been written) continues to the present, and beyond, describing events, nations and characters, as they impinge on the people of God. We can learn about each in turn.

Since a large part of *Revelation* deals with the demise of the Roman Empire and later political religious bodies, if this were set out in plain language, it would have been the cause of far greater persecution of Christians within the empire, and that was already severe enough to be a disgrace to its memory. When the Reformers revealed that secret there was more fierce persecution from the same quarter of all who believed and understood this prophecy, and persecutions continue to this day.

Despite the sense of mystery that surrounds *Revelation*, it is kind to those who observe it, being mainly chronological in its form, with passages in parenthesis to explain or expand its theme as needed; like any well written drama, it alternates between the fortunes of the good, and the bad.

It is vital to approach *Revelation* with an open and prayerful mind, avoiding and setting aside, if need be, previously-held forms of theological correctness, just letting Christ's own words and history reveal the clarity of this vivid vision.

As the Lord Jesus in His earthly ministry spoke of rewards and blessings for the faithful, so in *Revelation* He tells us of these tremendous blessings and does not shrink from warning of the fierce judgements coming with certainty on all who oppose His sovereign will.

Michael Jarvis

(NB: all biblical references are to the Authorised King James Version)

Chapter 1

1 v. 1-3. The Revelation of Jesus Christ, which God gave unto him, to shew unto his servants things which must shortly come to pass; and he sent and signified it by his angel unto his servant John:

Who bare record of the word of God, and of the testimony of Jesus Christ, and of all things that he saw.

Blessed is he that readeth, and they that hear the words of this prophecy, and keep those things which are written therein: for the time is at hand.

The first thing we notice is that God is the author of this prophecy, Who gave it to Jesus, so that He would pass it on to us. It is urgent, concerning things about to occur, and things are still about to occur now. John explains that he is only the secretary recording it for us. There is immediately a blessing for those that will read or hear this message. Are you ready to receive His blessing by taking this message for your guidance?

1 v. 4-8. John to the seven churches which are in Asia: Grace be unto you, and peace, from him which is, and which was, and which is to come; and from the seven Spirits that are before his throne;

And from Jesus Christ, who is the faithful witness, and the first begotten of the dead, and the prince of the kings of the earth. Unto him that loved us, and washed us from our sins in his own blood,

And hath made us kings and priests unto God and his Father; to him be glory and dominion for ever and ever. Amen.

Behold, he cometh with clouds; and every eye shall see him, and they also which pierced him: and all kindreds of the earth shall wail because of him. Even so. Amen.

I am Alpha and Omega, the beginning and the ending, saith the Lord, which is, and which was, and which is to come, the Almighty.

John explains that he is sending this Revelation to the seven churches, and recites the credentials and authority of Jesus, his master, as was the secretarial custom for letter writing in those days.

1 v. 9-10. I John, who also am your brother, and companion in tribulation, and in the kingdom and patience of Jesus Christ, was in the isle that is called Patmos, for the word of God, and for the testimony of Jesus Christ.

I was in the Spirit on the Lord's Day, and heard behind me a great voice, as of a trumpet.

As we approach *Revelation*, we too need like John to be in the Spirit, in order that Jesus may speak to us, and hearing His voice to give us understanding.

1 v. 11-18. Saying, I am Alpha and Omega, the first and the last: and, What thou seest, write in a book, and send it unto the seven churches which are in Asia; unto Ephesus, and unto Smyrna, and unto Pergamos, and unto Thyatira, and unto Sardis, and unto Philadelphia, and unto Laodicea.

And I turned to see the voice that spake with me. And being turned, I saw seven golden candlesticks;

And in the midst of the seven candlesticks one like unto the Son of man, clothed with a garment down to the foot, and girt about the paps with a golden girdle.

His head and his hairs were white like wool, as white as snow; and his eyes were as a flame of fire; and his feet like unto fine brass, as if they burned in a furnace; and his voice as the sound of many waters.

And he had in his right hand seven stars: and out of his mouth went a sharp two edged sword: and his countenance was as the sun shineth in his strength.

And when I saw him, I fell at his feet as dead. And he laid his right hand upon me, saying unto me, Fear not: I am the first and the last:

I am he that liveth, and was dead; and, behold, I am alive for evermore, Amen; and have the keys of hell and of death.

This vision develops rather like a choreographed script for a play, the scene changes as each character comes on stage and acts out his part. As each scene is presented, John's and our viewpoint is moved on in place and time; so that each is seen as if in the present, or near present. In this way Revelation is always up to date with current events. Here we see the hero, Christ at work among His people, through the agency and witness of His churches. Poor John is so awed at the sight, that he falls in a dead faint, and has to be revived and reassured by the Lord Jesus, before he can receive and record the vision. It is important to note that the golden girdle round Christ's heart is symbolic, telling us that although some of His duties are unpleasant, all that He does is out of love for His people and creation as a whole.

1 v. 19-20. Write the things which thou hast seen, and the things which are, and things which shall be hereafter;

The mystery of the seven stars which thou sawest in my right hand, and the seven golden candlesticks. The seven stars are the angels of the seven churches: and the seven candlesticks which thou sawest are the seven churches.

Here is the command for John to write, and two new symbols are explained for us. Candlesticks represent churches, those stars are their angels or messengers of the churches.

Chapter 2

2 v. 1-7. Unto the angel of the church of Ephesus write; These things saith he that holdeth the seven stars in his right hand, who walketh in the midst of the seven golden candlesticks;

I know thy works, and thy labour, and thy patience, and how thou canst not bear them which are evil: and thou hast tried them which say they are apostles, and are not, and hast found them liars:

And hast borne, and hast patience, and for my name's sake hast laboured, and hast not fainted.

Nevertheless I have somewhat against thee, because thou hast left thy first love.

Remember therefore from whence thou art fallen, and repent, and do the first works; or else I will come unto thee quickly, and will remove thy candlestick out of his place, except thou repent.

But this thou hast, that thou hatest the deeds of the Nicolaitanes, which I also hate.

He that hath an ear, let him hear what the Spirit saith unto the churches; To him that overcometh will I give to eat of the tree of life, which is in the midst of the paradise of God.

Ephesus; a church visited by Paul, where he preached for three months in the synagogue, and then in the school of Tyrannus for a further two years; what a seminar! It seems to have been a good church that for some reason, possibly because they ejected Paul, (*Acts* 19) had deviated from its first principles, yet it still had good points. The reason is not obvious, but it may have been a loss of faith when the possible expected return of Christ to rescue Jerusalem from destruction by Titus in AD 70 did not take place; or perhaps they were very modern in allowing their Christian status to obscure their Israelite origins and covenant responsibilities. There were many from the dispersed Ten Tribes from Asia to Asia Minor, and beyond, a factor that influenced the disciples to visit such places and set up churches; for Jesus had said '*Go to the lost sheep...*'

The Nicolaitanes were unpopular there, which pleased our Lord. If they were the followers of someone called Nicolas, we do not know what he did to become unpopular. On the other hand it may be a composite word from two Greek words meaning to have power over the laity, being a power- hungry priestly sect, quite contrary to Christ's teaching of humility in service.

The message concludes with a wonderful promise to the faithful.

Although these are historic churches, in the prophetic sense each church represents by its characteristics, not only itself as it then was, but in addition a period of church history, this church represents a church history period from about AD 35 – 100.

2 v. 8-11. And unto the angel of the church in Smyrna write; These things saith the first and the last, which was dead and is alive;

I know thy works, and tribulation, and poverty, (but thou art rich) and I know the blasphemy of them which say they are Jews, and are not, but are the synagogue of Satan.

Fear none of those things which thou shalt suffer: behold, the devil shall cast some of you into prison, that ye may be tried; and ye shall have tribulation ten days: be thou faithful unto death, and I will give thee a crown of life.

He that hath an ear, let him hear what the Spirit saith unto the churches; He that overcometh shall not be hurt of the second death.

Smyrna; Jesus reminds this church that He is the Risen Saviour. The synagogue of Satan is of those who claimed to be Jews, were anti Christian, joining the church to pervert it. As far back as the time of Ezra and Nehemiah there were those who returned to Jerusalem that were not really Jews, and were barred from holding office. And in the First Centuries BC and AD there were those who under the Herods, joined the Jews but were Idumeans. At the destruction of Jerusalem these would have been dispersed and looking for synagogues in fresh places. Let those who hold that the Jewish and Christian faiths have so much in common take note of these things, Jesus did not mention this without good reason.

The ten days, on the *Revelation* time scale of a day for a year, represents the Diocletian persecution of AD 303-313, which was brought to an end when Constantine, a British prince, became emperor and promoted the status of Christians. Their unrecognised riches were the large numbers who died for their faith at that time to become the overcomers, who are immune to the second death, because they are alive in Christ who ever lives.

Smyrna represents the church history period from about AD 100-313.

2 v. 12-17. And to the angel of the church in Pergamos write; These things saith he which hath the sharp sword with two edges;

I know thy works, and where thou dwellest, even where Satan's seat is: and thou holdest fast my name, and hast not denied my faith, even in those days wherein Antipas was my faithful martyr, who was slain among you, where Satan dwelleth.

But I have a few things against thee, because thou hast there them that hold the doctrine of Balaam, who taught Balac to cast a stumbling block before the children of Israel, to eat things sacrificed unto idols, and to commit fornication.

So hast thou also them that hold the doctrine of the Nicolaitanes, which thing I hate.

Repent; or else I will come unto thee quickly, and will fight against them with the sword of my mouth.

He that hath an ear, let him hear what the Spirit saith unto the churches; To him that overcometh will I give to eat of the hidden manna, and will give him a white stone, and in the stone a new name written, which no man knoweth saving he that receiveth it.

Pergamos; there are many, probably most, names that have meanings. This name means 'married to power'. Constantine, no doubt with the best of intentions, being emperor and a Christian, gave Christians and the church special protection during his reign; so much so that it became incorporated into, or owned by the state, and not reliant on Christ and guided by the Holy Spirit. That is why it is said to dwell 'where Satan's seat is'. As will become clear later the Roman earth is the object of God's wrath and judgement, the place for his church to witness, but not to become an integral part. It was a union between Christ's church and extreme worldliness. This led to the corruption of the Gospel message.

Because of its political connections, it became power loving, with an over powerful priestly authority soon taking charge. Some clearly resisted this development, and are commended for their faithfulness, and kept safe in Jesus receiving His manna to sustain them, and His white stone, symbolic of their being an integral part of God's Kingdom represented as a growing or living stone in Nebuchadnezzar's dream of *Daniel* 2, so confirming that Kingdom message as being a proper and vital part of church teaching and objective.

This church represents the church of AD 313-606.

2 v. 18-29. And unto the angel of the church in Thyatira write; These things saith the Son of God, who hath his eyes like unto a flame of fire, and his feet are like fine brass;

I know thy works, and charity, and service, and faith, and thy patience, and thy works; and the last to be more than the first.

Notwithstanding I have a few things against thee, because thou sufferest that woman Jezebel, which callest herself a prophetess, to teach and to seduce my servants to commit fornication, and to eat things sacrificed unto idols.

I gave her space to repent of her fornication; and she repented not. Behold, I will cast her into a bed, and them that commit adultery with her into great tribulation, except they repent of their deeds.

And I will kill her children with death; and all the churches shall know that I am he which searcheth the reins and hearts: and I will give unto every one of you according to your works.

But unto you I say, and unto the rest in Thyatira, as many as have not this doctrine, and which have not known the depths of Satan, as they speak; I will put upon you none other burden.

But that which ye have already hold fast till I come.

And he that overcometh, and keepeth my works unto the end, to him will I give power over the nations:
And he shall rule them with a rod of iron; as the vessels of a potter shall they be broken to shivers: even as I received from my Father.

And I will give him the morning star.

*He that hath an ear, let him hear what the Spirit saith unto the
churches.*

Thyatira; it means 'ruled by a woman', her identity will be more
clearly seen and her destiny dealt with much later. Like Queen Jezebel
caused Israel to worship idols, so does this woman lead the churches into
idolatry. There is the unheeded call to repentance, and the warning of
catastrophe to follow.

There is a promise to those who resist corruption and do not lower
their standards; they will be given authority over nations in time to come.
This church shows the condition of the church dominated by Rome in
what are called the 'dark middle ages' from about AD 606 – 1860s, the
period of Papal supremacy.

Chapter 3

3 v. 1- 6. And unto the angel of the church in Sardis write; These things saith he that hath the seven Spirits of God, and the seven stars; I know thy works, that thou hast a name that thou livest, and art dead.

Be watchful, and strengthen the things which remain, that are ready to die: for I have not found thy works perfect before God.

Remember therefore how thou hast received and heard, and hold fast, and repent. If therefore thou shalt not watch, I will come on thee as a thief, and thou shalt not know what hour I will come upon thee.

Thou hast a few names even in Sardis which have not defiled their garments; and they shall walk with me in white: for they are worthy.

He that overcometh, the same shall be clothed in white raiment; and I will not blot out his name out of the book of life, but I will confess his name before my Father, and before his angels.

He that hath an ear let him hear what the Spirit saith unto the churches.

Sardis; a very sad state of affairs, the true gospel is nearly lost, yet there is a bright light in that darkened place. Sardis church was very much alive to the world but nearly dead to God. Another invitation to repent is offered to the nominally Christian Roman Church, from within which a few faithful souls started the Reformation. They were trying to bring the church back to the true teaching of the Bible, and Jesus will reward them for their witness, but Rome rejected them. Tremendous effort despite extreme opposition went into translating the Bible into English and other languages, and it became better known and more widely read than for centuries.

The Sardis church represents the period from about AD 1360s – 1600s.

3 v. 7-13. And to the angel of the church in Philadelphia write; These things saith he that is holy, he that is true, he that hath the key of David, he that openeth and no man shutteth; and shutteth and no man openeth;

I know thy works: behold, I have set before thee an open door, and no man can shut it: for thou hast a little strength, and hast kept my word, and hast not denied my name.

Behold, I will make them of the synagogue of Satan, which say they are Jews, and are not, but do lie; behold, I will make them to come and worship before thy feet, and to know that I have loved thee.

Because thou hast kept the word of my patience, I also will keep thee from the hour of temptation, which shall come upon all the world, to try them that dwell upon the earth.

Behold I come quickly: hold that fast which thou hast, that no man take thy crown.

Him that overcometh will I make a pillar in the temple of my God, and he shall go no more out: and I will write upon him the name of my God, and the name of the city of my God, which is new Jerusalem, which cometh down out of heaven from my God: and I will write upon him my new name.

He that hath an ear, let him hear what the Spirit saith unto the churches.

Philadelphia; or the love of a brother. The reference to the key of David is a marker denoting that the open door was for the development of the Reformed Church, under the patronage of David's descendants Henry VIII, Elizabeth I and James I and their successors, independent of and distinct from the Roman Church. After a period of Church of England conformity, other nonconformist churches developed, and nothing was able to prevent this, for the door had been opened. It was a time of liberation and expansion of the gospel of Christ.

The early settlers in America, understood this, and declared their freedom under God in their State Charters and Constitutions, and made their capital at Philadelphia from 1790 until 1800.

The verse 9, Jews that are not, is like Smyrna, where they attempted to subvert the church from within; but in this case it is symbolic language for the Roman Church subverting the Reformed Church from within, a process that has continued until the present. In both cases it is the old faith trying to overcome the new, the opportunity to learn and repent being firmly rejected. There is a warning of severe testing times, and reward for those who remain faithful to Christ.

Philadelphia represents church history from about AD 1550s - 1800.

3 v. 14-19. And unto the angel of the church of the Laodiceans write; These things saith the Amen, the faithful and true witness, the beginning of the creation of God:

I know thy works, that thou art neither cold nor hot: I would thou wert cold or hot.

So then because thou art lukewarm, and neither cold nor hot, I will spue thee out of my mouth. Because thou sayest, I am rich and increased with goods, and have need of nothing: and knowest not that thou art wretched, and miserable, and poor, and blind, and naked:

I counsel thee to buy of me gold tried in the fire, that thou mayest be rich; and white raiment, that thou mayest be clothed, and that the shame of thy nakedness do not appear; and anoint thine eyes with eyesalve, that thou mayest see.

As many as I love, I rebuke and chasten: be zealous therefore, and repent.

Laodicea; The subversion of the Reformed Churches has continued since the Reformation, slowly and quietly for the most part, but has now progressed to the point that truth is often indistinguishable from error. The Protestant churches and denominations softened up, are now accepting Roman teachings as their clergy are indoctrinated by Roman sympathisers in their colleges, or are using the format of administration and authority of that type, instead of the humility in leadership taught by our Lord, which is now rare. All these things being stages in the process of bringing all denominations back to the Roman fold. Almost anything goes now so long so long as it is not the pure teaching of Bible truth. The truth is still there, and always will be, it cannot be destroyed or completely hidden, but you may find that you have to search for it; if you know its author you will be able to identify it, and know it, and proclaim it. Jesus still loves His Church, but warns that they should heed His rebuke and repent.

Will His warning be heeded, or do we have to move on to the final scene of this the first Act of this drama?

3 v. 20-22. Behold I stand at the door, and knock: if any man hear my voice, and open the door, I will come in to him, and will sup with him, and he with me.

To him that overcometh will I grant to sit with me in my throne, even as I also overcame, and am set down with my Father in his throne.

He that hath an ear, let him hear what the Spirit saith unto the churches.

If the warnings, and calls to repentance by our Saviour are ignored, if the dross and arrogance of humanism, and the worship of what we choose cannot be given up, for Christ's pure gold; then unlike the first scene of this drama where the Risen Christ is seen among His churches, we see Him shut outside. Even so, in love he is still seeking admission, that He might forgive and restore, and recover all that are lost or have been misled to a full and close harmony with Himself.

What an indictment and disgrace, especially as Christ warned of these developments so long ago. What love and compassion He still shows us, despite the many rebuffs, and will continue to do so, for He does not change.

We may well ask what has church leadership been up to for 1900 years that we should have arrived at this point?

Jesus said, '... *when the Son of man cometh, shall he find faith on the earth? (Luke* 18 v 8).

Chapter 4

4 v. 1-3. After this I looked, and, behold, a door was opened in heaven: and the first voice which I heard was as it were a trumpet talking with me; which said, Come up hither, and I will show thee things which must be hereafter.

And immediately I was in the spirit: and behold, a throne was set in heaven, and one sat on the throne.

And he that sat was to look upon like a jasper and a sardine stone: and there was a rainbow round about the throne, in sight like unto an emerald.

John is now in the spirit in heaven, the command 'to come up hither' places him close to the stage, or dais of the heavenly throne. From that position we shall later see him drawn into some parts of the drama that unfolds before our eyes, he is in a sense our representative, for it is us that God wants to involve in His purposes. He describes it all for our benefit, the enthroned Godhead, the rainbow to represent God's covenant keeping character. It must have been a great unexpected shock to John finding himself face to face with God, only possible through his faith in Jesus.

4 v. 4-5. And round about the throne were four and twenty seats: and upon the seats I saw four and twenty elders sitting, clothed in white raiment; and they had on their heads crowns of gold.

And out of the throne proceeded lightnings and thunderings and voices: and there were seven lamps of fire burning before the throne, which are the seven Spirits of God.

The twenty four elders may be like a double representation of the twelve Apostles who will judge the tribes of Israel, Matthew 19 v. 28. Their function seems to be the leading of the paeans of praise that occur as certain things are revealed. The lightning, thunder, voices and lamps demonstrate the lively and commanding nature of God.

4 v. 6-11. And before the throne there was a sea of glass like unto crystal: and in the midst of the throne, and round about the throne, were four beasts full of eyes before and behind.

And the first beast was like a lion, and the second beast like a calf, and the third beast had a face as a man, and the fourth beast was like a flying eagle.

And the four beasts had each of them six wings about him; and they were full of eyes within: and they rest not day and night, saying, Holy, holy, holy, Lord God Almighty, which was, and is, and is to come.

And when those beasts give glory and honour and thanks to him that sat on the throne, who liveth for ever and ever.

The four and twenty elders fall down before him that sat on the throne, and worship him that liveth for ever and ever, and cast their crowns before the throne, saying,

Thou art worthy, O Lord, to receive glory and honour and power: for thou hast created all things, and for thy pleasure they are and were created.

The sea of crystal or glass, is a vitally important feature of the heavenly structure, and of this series of visions. The all important characteristic of glass is that you can see through it, also it has a good reflecting surface. It shows or allows to be seen how events in the heavenly sphere can be discerned as having related events in the earth. Because the floor of heaven is depicted as if made of glass, by the eye of faith we are able to perceive the actions and glory of God; likewise God is able from his throne to observe the affairs of men, and influence them according to His will. As will be seen from where John was placed, he was able to see the events described in the heavenly sense, and by looking through the glass floor to observe the outworking of them on earth. It is similar to seeing from a suitable point the fish swimming in the pond or river, and at the same time to see the fisherman on the far bank trying to catch them; the two scenes become one.

There may be a connection between the appearance of the four beasts, as their heads or faces are given the same forms as the emblems or standards of the tribes of Israel that were stationed at the four cardinal positions round the tabernacle in the wilderness, for Moses was told by God to prepare everything according to the patterns shown him on Sinai. (*Exodus* 25 v. 9 & *Numbers* 8 v. 4). This teaches us that earthly things must be made to conform to the heavenly pattern. Revelation shows us a great deal of how this will be brought about, probably more so than any other single book in the Bible.

There is a lot happening here, there is something resembling an oratorio within this vision, for events are interspersed with a chorus singing the praises of God, and the hero of the vision Christ, a frequent reminder of His worthiness. This vision of pre-enactment of earthly events is about to begin with the obvious purpose of showing to John, and hence also to us, that God's will is done on earth, as in heaven, for which Our Lord Jesus taught us to pray. The whole of this vision of heaven and its activities, have some prophetic sense of displaying the future orderly rule of Christ to be established on the earth. This fact may well be at least a part of the blessing promised to those who read Revelation, to see that despite many things that seem to be to the contrary, God's will is being done. By observing events of their own day, Christ's followers have been, and still are able to discover how God's programme is advancing. This is why Revelation's vision is so important, and why it is so sad that so few Christians bother with it. Solomon, the wisest of men wrote, 'Where there is no vision, the people perish'. (*Proverbs* 29 v. 18). That is why in this study every part of the vision is read in full, and is always more important than the comments made about it.

Chapter 5

5 v. 1. And I saw in the right hand of him that sat on the throne a book written within and on the backside, sealed with seven seals.

John sees in God's hand a book or scroll, unusual because it is sealed with seven seals, so arranged that only a portion may be read until the next seal is removed.

5 v. 2-4. And I saw a strong angel proclaiming with a loud voice, Who is worthy to open the book, and to loose the seals thereof?

And no man in heaven, nor in earth, neither under the earth, was able to open the book, neither to look thereon.

And I wept much, because no man was found worthy to open and read the book, neither to look thereon.

John is distressed as it first appears that no one in heaven or earth can open the book.

5 v. 5-7. And one of the elders saith unto me, Weep not: behold, the Lion of the tribe of Juda, the Root of David, hath prevailed to open the book, and loose the seven seals thereof.

And I beheld, and, lo, in the midst of the throne and of the four beasts, and in the midst of the elders, stood a Lamb as it had been slain, having seven horns and seven eyes, which are the seven Spirits of God sent forth into all the earth.

And he came and took the book out of the right hand of him that sat upon the throne.

John, because he is shown, now notices the Lamb, alive, yet with the marks showing it had been sacrificed. Right in front of God's throne is the witness that Jesus died to save us from our sins, and that our redemption is secure. Notice the seven horns; horns represent Kingship. (*Daniel* 7 v. 24.)

The Lamb takes the book, He is the One worthy to do this.

5 v. 8-10. And when he had taken the book, the four beasts and four and twenty elders fell down before the Lamb, having every one of them harps, and golden vials full of odours, which are the prayers of the saints. And they sung a new song, saying, Thou art worthy to take the book, and to open the seals thereof: for thou wast slain, and hast redeemed us to God by thy blood out of every kindred, and tongue, and people, and nation;

And hast made us unto our God kings and priests: and we shall reign on the earth.

To mark the importance of this there is a suitable act of worship and praise. This includes the parading of the prayers of the saints before the throne of God, as if they are reminding Him that they are awaiting His judgement on all that the Bible calls Babylon.

5 v. 11-14.   And I beheld, and I heard the voice of many angels round about the throne and the beasts and the elders: and the number of them was ten thousand times ten thousand, and thousands of thousands;

Saying with a loud voice, Worthy is the Lamb that was slain to receive power, and riches, and wisdom, and strength, and honour, and glory, and blessing.

And every creature which is in heaven, and on the earth, and under the earth, and such as are in the sea, and all that are in them, heard I saying, Blessing, and honour, and glory, and power, be unto him that sitteth upon the throne, and unto the Lamb for ever and ever. And the four beasts said, Amen. And the four and twenty elders fell down and worshipped him that liveth for ever and ever.

John became aware of an enormous gathering who joined in this paean of praise, the auditorium of heaven is vast, with spaces for very many millions. He also through the glass floor saw praises from earth.

It is said that the universe is expanding, if so heaven may also be expanding, as there is no limit to the infinite power of God. This scene is the inspiration for part of Handel's Messiah.

Chapter 6

6 v. 1-2. And I saw when the Lamb opened one of the seals, and I heard, as it were the noise of thunder, one of the four beasts saying, Come and see.

And I saw, and behold a white horse: and he that sat on him had a bow; and a crown was given unto him: and he went forth conquering, and to conquer.

Imagine the hush in that great heavenly host, the moment of anticipation and expectancy as the Lamb of God prepares to break the first seal. It snaps in his hand. He unrolls the scroll until the second seal prevents further movement. John is bidden to come close to see, In his vision he steps forward to see the contents of the scroll, right up close to Jesus, who shows him what is written and drawn on the exposed part of the scroll. The white horse and rider, wearing a crown or laurel wreath, and carrying a bow, is in the act of conquering. It represents the Roman Empire in the arrogance of its heyday, full of confidence and doing just about anything it pleased. Some have supposed that this picture represents Christ, but He is shown with a two-edged sword as His weapon. This is more evident when we see the following sections of the vision, as being the first of a naturally occurring sequence of historic events, into which Christ the conquering hero does not fit. Christ is the conqueror of sin and death. This rider is the cause of untold suffering and death. This vision represents the condition of the Roman Empire or earth at the time when John saw and recorded the vision in about AD 90, until about AD 180.

6 v. 3-4. And when he had opened the second seal, I heard the second beast say. Come and see. And there went out another horse that was red: and power was given to him that sat thereon to take peace from the earth, and that they should kill one another: and there was given unto him a great sword.

The opening of the second seal prompts another invitation to, Come and see. The description of this red horse going out, implies motion. Thus the vision is one of the spoken Word together with motion pictures, exactly as we experience a film or video; The Word of God is always up to date, and can address us in terms that we understand. This is a pre-enactment, and is seen to be actually happening, as also the act of giving the sword to the horseman, and its effect on the Roman earth or empire. The sword took peace from the Empire as civil wars, and unrest (killing and robbing their own people as distinct to conquering others as seen with the white horse) resulted from rivals ruthlessly seeking power for its own sake, from about AD 185 - 284.

6 v. 5-6. And when he had opened the third seal, I heard the third beast say, Come and see. And I beheld, and lo a black horse; and he that sat on him had a pair of balances in his hand.

And I heard a voice in the midst of the four beasts say, A measure of wheat for a penny, and three measures of barley for a penny; and see thou hurt not the oil and the wine.

Enter the black horse with rider and balances. The repeated instruction to John to 'Come and see' seems to imply that once he had seen that particular section he retired to his former position near the open door to heaven, to await the Lamb of God opening the next seal. The high cost of civil war has to be paid for. The damage to the economy in loss of life and manpower. That most basic industry of food production is greatly affected, and there is not enough production to meet even basic needs. The government's answer to the problem is to increase taxation. To balance the books and give the latest Emperor all that he demands, tax officials took just about everything including seed reserved to sow for next seasons harvest. These events occur during the latter part of the period of civil unrest and are caused by it. The greed within the controlling forces of the empire reduces vast numbers to beggary from about AD 202-250. And so we move on to the next part of the vision.

6 v. 7- 8. And when he had opened the fourth seal, I heard the voice of the fourth beast say, Come and see.

And I looked, and behold a pale horse: and his name that sat on him was Death, and Hell followed with him. And power was given unto them over the fourth part of the earth, to kill with the sword, and with hunger, and with death, and with the beasts of the earth.

The pale horse of Death shows the inevitable course of events that must follow so great an abuse of temporal power. Famine, disease, plague, neglect and death, even the dogs were eating from unburied corpses. Gibbon states that, *'A furious plague raged from AD 265, --- in every province --- consumed in a few years half the human species'.* The early Church historian Eusebius describes this period in similar words.

About AD 250 - 300 is represented by the fourth seal.

6 v. 9-11. And when he had opened the fifth seal, I saw under the altar the souls of them that were slain for the word of God, and for the testimony which they held:

And they cried with a loud voice, saying, How long, O Lord, holy and true, dost thou not judge and avenge our blood on them that dwell on the earth?

And white robes were given unto every one of them: and it was said unto them, that they should rest for a little season, until their fellow servants also and their brethren, that should be killed as they were, should be fulfilled.

The fifth seal reveals the many martyrs of the Christian Church. They are asking the Lamb to judge and punish the Roman earth. It should be noted that throughout Revelation the earth is the Roman sphere of influence, and at that time all persecution of Christians was within the empire; even persecution by Jews had been within the empire. This refers particularly to the Diocletian persecution of AD 303-313. And they were told that although that persecution was now past, the true church of Jesus Christ would have to face further persecutions by Rome, or other powers, and more would be added to their numbers. The gift of white robes is a token, to show that those who were faithful unto death, will rise in glory and reign with Christ at His return.

We have seen the decline of the Roman empire in its pagan form, its total disregard for human life, as the most efficient killing machine the world had then known, and we could say that its end was well deserved. It should also be seen as a breach of Natural Law, and common sense tells us that disaster must follow such excesses: these disasters are the judgement of God, as becomes clearer in the next sections.

6 v. 12-17. And I beheld when he had opened the sixth seal, and, lo, there was a great earthquake; and the sun became black as sackcloth of hair, and the moon became as blood;

And the stars of heaven fell unto the earth, even as a fig tree casteth her untimely figs, when she is shaken of a mighty wind.

And the heaven departed as a scroll when it is rolled together; and every mountain and island were moved out of their places.

And the kings of the earth, and the great men, and the rich men, and the chief captains, and the mighty men, and every bondman, and every free man, hid themselves in the dens and in the rock of the mountains;

And said to the mountains and rocks, Fall on us, and hide us from the face of him that sitteth on the throne, and from the wrath of the Lamb:

For the great day of his wrath is come; and who shall be able to stand?

The sixth seal reveals a massive upheaval within the empire. Constantine, a British prince, became Emperor, he was also a Christian. The old ideas that the emperor was god, were made to give way to him being the 'Executive Agent of God'. He tolerated no persecution of Christians, that had marked the reign of his predecessor Diocletian. His action is well symbolised as an earthquake, with wind and heaven being like a scroll suddenly rolled up; for at a stroke he removed all officials from their office who were pagans and opposed to the Christian Church. In their place he appointed Christians. Like many well intended decisions and laws, it was good in the short term but bad in the long term. Persecution was ended. Rich and poor, bond and free, if you were a pagan your world had ended, there was no hiding place and no security for you. Except of course in the Church, where converts were always welcomed. Many saw this as a way out of the dilemma. Those who wanted to keep their position became instant Christians. The Church became married to the State, as we saw in the letter to the Church at Pergamos.

Constantine by choosing to have his own capital at Constantinople as well as Rome, prepared the way for the division of the empire and the church. A legacy of this is seen in the Roman Catholic and the Eastern Orthodox Churches.

Some saw this as a judgement of God on paganism: but imagine the effect on the Church. The Church had now the protection of the emperor, but was inundated with those who wanted to hold on to their lucrative positions. The greater part of the civil service, army officers, and judiciary, and doubtless a number of pagan priests, wanted to join the

Church. Unfortunately, this was not because they were repentant of their sins, or were committed to the Lord Jesus, to anything beyond the least possible degree, but for worldly advantage. They saw membership of the Church as a means to an end, they saw to it that its spiritual motivation was adulterated for political expediency that would help to advance their position and authority. Indeed they could use their influence to obtain the sanction of the Church, and so make any act or policy seem right and as having God's blessing.

It is not hard to see how the Roman Church incorporated an authoritarian priesthood, the worship of Mary, images, and various non-biblical doctrines into its beliefs, it didn't have a lot of choice, it was power first, and never mind the truth, we are right because we say so. It was a great, but missed opportunity for Rome to repent, but rather than submit to Christ they thought to manipulate Him to submit to them. This sixth seal represents the period from AD 313 to about 395.

At this point *Revelation* breaks off the chronological sequence, to observe what God is doing for and with His people, Israel, in their wanderings to fulfil His purposes for them. We return at a later point to the seventh seal.

There is also a longer term aspect to this prophecy, for these days. It looks forward to a greater judgement on Rome, sometimes referred to as Babylon that is described in a later chapter. The cataclysmic events of which will send the rich and powerful running to their bunkers. Many are the 'secret' safe, even safe against nuclear attack, installations that have been prepared to protect elite government personnel, and communication systems. One wonders what they will do when they emerge from these dens in the rocks in the event of such attacks and find everyone dead and the whole land a desert, to whom will they go to buy their caviar and chips, and gin and tonics?

Chapter 7

7 v. 1- 3. And after these things I saw four angels standing on the four corners of the earth, holding the four winds of the earth, that the wind should not blow on the earth, nor on the sea, nor on any tree.

And I saw another angel ascending from the east, having the seal of the living God; and he cried with a loud voice to the four angels, to whom it was given to hurt the earth and the sea,

Saying, Hurt not the earth, neither the sea, nor the trees, till we have sealed the servants of our God in their foreheads.

These four angels represent God's power to cause chaos within the Roman Empire, they are told not to do that for the time being, causing a period of calm in the empire. We are clearly told the purpose, to seal or secure the well being of God's servant people, to put them in a position of relative security away from the further judgements on the Roman earth, when the seventh seal is later opened. It was an opportunity to do then, as they are later told again in *Revelation* 18 v 4, 'Come out of her, my people, that ye be not partakers of her sins, and that ye receive not of her plagues'.

7 v. 4-8. And I heard the number of them which were sealed: and there were sealed an hundred and forty and four thousand of all the tribes of the children of Israel.

Of the tribe of Juda were sealed twelve thousand. Of the tribe of Reuben were sealed twelve thousand. Of the tribe of Gad were sealed twelve thousand.

Of the tribe of Aser were sealed twelve thousand. Of the tribe of Nepthalim were sealed twelve thousand.

Of the tribe of Manasses were sealed twelve thousand.

Of the tribe of Simeon were sealed twelve thousand. Of the tribe of Levi were sealed twelve thousand. Of the tribe of Issachar were sealed twelve thousand.

Of the tribe of Zabulon were sealed twelve thousand. Of the tribe of Joseph were sealed twelve thousand. Of the tribe of Benjamin were sealed twelve thousand.

It could hardly be more plainly stated. This cannot possibly refer to the Jews alone, nor to the Christian church who had already incorporated persons of every nation within the empire and beyond its limits, but Manasses being part of Joseph's tribe gets a seemingly extra mention. This may not be the intended meaning, as Ephraim already had the birthright, given to him by Jacob, and was counted as equal to or in place of Joseph, and so Manasses needed to be included to make up the twelve, but is actually the thirteenth tribe.

The omission of Dan is generally regarded as a scribal error, yet it may reflect the fact that Dan was much into shipping, ('...why did Dan remain in ships...'*Judges* 5 v.17) and heavily involved with the Phoenician alliance, and therefore more mobile than the other tribes, and less influenced by unhappy conditions within the empire. Dan may have already become settled in the British Isles, either before, or after the Roman legions had withdrawn. In either case, if it is an error we should assume the intention that Dan was also protected by the seal, or alternatively, Dan was already beyond the power of Rome, and so did not require the protection of the seal.

The number of sealed ones being equal for each tribe, implies not a literal number but symbolic of God's intended future wholeness and completeness of His people. It is a fact of history that great numbers entered Britain after the departure of Roman power. They quarrelled over their new found inheritance, as sometimes members of a family are prone to do, and took centuries to become officially unified.

This process is the fulfilment of the promise to King David, (II *Samuel* 7 v. 10) where it was stated that God would provide and move Israel to a new land.

7 v. 9-12. After this I beheld , and, lo, a great multitude, which no man could number, of all nations, and kindreds, and people, and tongues, stood before the throne, and before the Lamb, clothed in white robes, and palms in their hands:

And cried with a loud voice, saying, Salvation to our God which sitteth upon the throne, and unto the Lamb.

And all the angels stood round about the throne, and about the elders and the four beasts, and fell before the throne on their faces, and worshipped God,

Saying, Amen: Blessing, and glory, and wisdom, and thanksgiving, and honour, and power, and might, be unto our God for ever and ever. Amen.

John not only seeing and hearing these things in the heavenly enactment, can also see through heaven's glass floor, that the period of calm within the empire allowed the so called lost tribes of Israel to move freely to their appointed place. The inclusion of twelve named tribes is in keeping with the historic record that parts of Judah's and Benjamin's fenced cities, were also captured by the Assyrians, and so never went to or returned from Babylon. (*Isaiah* 36 v. 1). He sees them as having embraced the Christian faith, as was established by Joseph of Arimathea as early as AD 37, long before the church in Rome became contaminated with worldliness. In recognition of this, that august assembly around God's throne offer a further round of praise and thanksgiving. They can see that the true faith was already beginning to be sent out from Glastonbury. He notices too that many in that throng around the Throne are wearing white robes.

7 v. 13- 17. And one of the elders answered, saying unto me, What are these that are arrayed in white robes? And whence came they?

And I said unto him, Sir, thou knowest. And he said unto me, These are they which came out of great tribulation, and have washed their robes, and made them white in the blood of the Lamb.

Therefore they are before the throne of God, and serve him day and night in his temple: and he that sitteth on the throne shall dwell among them.

They shall hunger no more, neither thirst any more; neither shall the sun light on them, nor any heat.

For the Lamb which is in the midst of the throne shall feed them, and shall lead them unto living fountains of waters: and God shall wipe away all tears from their eyes.

John declines to give an answer to the questions, What are these that are arrayed in white robes? And whence came they? This is not surprising as he did not yet see or understand the future sufferings of those who followed Jesus. He was only exiled for his faith. He was seeing that those who according to the promise, had entered the new homeland, were accepting the Christian faith, formed their first church twenty or so years before Paul wrote to the churches in Asia; they were sending out evangelists who were even then suffering for their faith, and he was being shown their reward, to be forever with Christ and share in His glory. Would you or I have known what to say?

There are many misunderstandings about what happens to our dead Christian loved ones. This is because there are statements about the dead, that look only at the material and physical aspects. The body returns to the earth and the material elements from which we are made, it has no ability to know how long it has been dead, or remember anything. Yet John is shown the dead in Christ serving Him, in that heavenly temple. The spirit returns to God who gave it. The souls are the identity that is recorded in the Lamb's Book of Life on acceptance of Him as Saviour, not waiting for the resurrection before they can praise God, or meet with Jesus, their entry in that book records their praises, and they are in that eternal presence, where it is always now and unchanging because of elapsed time. When the Day of Resurrection comes, there will be no differences because of time and date of death, it will be the same for all, in a moment. Christ who has power over life and death, will, at the resurrection, raise and reconstitute the body in a different form to the present ones, but like His own, alive by a form of metabolism or power that we are not yet able to see or understand, except by the eye of faith.

We have been looking at the judgements of God with the opening of six of the seven seals on the pagan Roman empire; the sealing by God of the tribes of Israel for their security in Britain, and western Europe, and the servants of Jesus praising Him in heaven. Now we return to the seventh seal.

Chapter 8

8 v. 1. And when he had opened the seventh seal, there was silence in heaven about the space of half an hour.

The half hour silence relates to the four angels that were holding the four winds (7 v. 1) that is to say they curtailed the turbulent nature of the empire, that allowed the movement and sealing to take place.

Psalm 105 v. 13-14. When they went from one nation to another, from one kingdom to another people; He suffered no man to do them wrong: yea, he reproved kings for their sakes;

8 v.2. And I saw the seven angels which stood before God; and to them were given seven trumpets.

We are informed that the seventh seal is to be subdivided into seven trumpets, each of which in turn will be sounded by the seven angels.

8 v.3-4. And another angel came and stood at the altar, having a golden censer; and there was given unto him much incense, that he should offer it with the prayers of all saints upon the golden altar which was before the throne.

And the smoke of the incense, which came with the prayers of the saints, ascended up before God out of the angel's hand.

This "another angel" is probably none other than the Lord Jesus, officiating at the altar as our High Priest, our prayers being offered in His name. He is demonstrating that the prayers of the faithful are accepted and pleasing to God, and therefore will be answered. Many are the martyrs of Jesus, and others who have suffered in some way for the testimony of Jesus, who have waited long to see justice done, and this is an assurance that their prayers have been heard, and will be answered, for God has this matter in hand.

8 v.5. And the angel took the censer, and filled it with fire of the altar, and cast it into the earth: and there were voices, and thunderings, and lightnings, and an earthquake.

God sometimes speaks or answers with fire. He spoke to Moses from the burning bush. He expressed His deep displeasure by destructive fire on Aaron's sons. (*Leviticus* 10 v. 2). He answered Elijah and the priests of Baal with fire. He sends His Holy Spirit with fire. Here He is signifying impending judgement on the now divided (since AD 395) Roman empire. This is to commence about AD 400. This fire from heaven causes shock waves and panic throughout the Roman earth as unexpected troubles fall upon them.

8 v. 6-7. And the seven angels that had the seven trumpets prepared themselves to sound.

And the first angel sounded, and there followed hail and fire mingled with blood, and they were cast upon the earth: and the third part of trees was burnt up, and all green grass was burnt up.

Of the seven trumpet blasts the first four describe the destructive judgement of God on the Western part of the Roman empire by Gothic adventurers. The first waves of them led by Alaric, attacked Gaul, Spain and even Italy. So alarmed was Rome that the legions based in Britain were recalled to help protect the homeland. The empire now divided into East and West, was attacked on three fronts, the scorched earth tactics of Gothic invasions being the first third of territory to be destroyed about AD 400 – 410.

Whilst it is not a specific part of *Revelation's* message to explain the origin of the Goths and other tribal entities onto the European stage, a very brief account of who they were, and where they came from is a worthwhile diversion.

They emerged from Asia and Asia Minor by way of the Caucasus regions, hence they have been known as Caucasians to this very day, without the realisation of who they really were and are. They were seeking new homelands because of the collapse of the Parthian Empire* in which they had been the dominant peoples. They were composed largely of the descendants of Israelites that had been deported to those parts centuries earlier. It is strange that Biblical history records Israel being taken to the Caucasus and parts beyond the Euphrates, but secular history is unable to connect the Caucasians with those who had

---

* Collins, Steven M. *Parthia the Forgotten Ancient Super Power*, ISBN 0-9725849-2-7. Available from CPC, 121 Low Etherley, Bishop Auckland, Co. Durham DL14 0HA. Tel. 01388 835753. Also from Bible Blessings, PO Box 1778, Royal Oak, MI 48068. USA.

previously been taken to the same regions. By this means God was using His People in His judgements on Rome, sometimes called Babylon; as indicated in *Jeremiah* 51 v. 20.

8 v. 8- 9. And the second angel sounded, and as it were a great mountain burning with fire was cast into sea: and the third part of the sea became blood;

And the third part of the creatures which were in the sea, and had life, died; and the third part of the ships were destroyed.

The judgement covers a period from about AD 425 – 470. The Vandals under the leadership of Genseric, caused great havoc for Rome, and by way of piracy, destroyed shipping that was needed to supply the empire. They established themselves at Carthage and destroyed Rome's Mediterranean naval and merchant fleets. The Mediterranean Sea became completely dominated by Carthage, and any vessel afloat in those parts was in extreme danger. So great was the impact of these people that even today we use their name to describe acts of wanton destruction.

8 v. 10-11. And the third angel sounded, and there fell a great star from heaven, burning as it were a lamp, and it fell upon the third part of the rivers, and upon the fountains of waters:

And the name of the star was called Wormwood: and the third part of the waters became wormwood: and many men died of the waters, because they were made bitter.

A great or bright star symbolises a notable, powerful and forceful individual. In this case Attila the Hun, who, around the AD 450s devastated the fertile valleys of the Rhine, the Danube and the Po, so causing great loss of life and great hardship. The wormwood (sometimes with gall) signifies the bitterness of this loss to Rome and the empire because of interrupted food production. This was further judgement on Rome, which although now nominally Christian, remained proud and unrepentant. Attila the Hun has passed into history as the scourge of God; one wonders if that epitaph is what he thought himself to be!

8 v. 12-13. And the fourth angel sounded, and the third part of the sun was smitten, and the third part of the moon, and the third part of the stars; so as the third part of them was darkened, and the day shone not for a third part of it, and the night likewise.

And I beheld, and heard an angel flying through the midst of heaven, saying with a loud voice, Woe, woe, woe, to the inhabitants of the earth by reason of the other voices of the trumpet of the three angels, which are yet to sound!

The sun, moon and stars, being the brightest objects in the heavens, are symbolic here of Rome, itself the symbol and jewel of the empire. This judgement fell upon Rome when it was conquered by Odoacer and the Heruli, in AD 476, at that time the Emperor Romulus Angustus was banished.

As we watch the Roman empire being dissected and destroyed piece by piece, it is interesting to note that there is a similarity and consistency in the use of trumpets in the plans of God, for when in an earlier era God destroyed Jericho, it took seven days marching round using trumpets.

The symbols of earth, sea, rivers and sun, will occur again later, - watch out for them. Finally we are reminded that there are three more angels to sound their trumpets, and deliver the judgement of God.

There is only one way to avoid the judgement of God; it is by faith in the Lord Jesus Christ, by confession to Him and asking for His forgiveness and saving Grace.

Chapter 9

9 v. 1-2. And the fifth angel sounded, and I saw a star fall from heaven unto the earth: and to him was given the key to the bottomless pit.

And he opened the bottomless pit; and there arose a smoke out of the pit, as the smoke of a great furnace; and the sun and the air were darkened by reason of the smoke of the pit.

What is the star that fell from heaven? In *Revelation* heavenly bodies sometimes represent a notable person. In *Luke* 10 v. 18 Jesus said, 'I beheld Satan as lightning fall from heaven'. From that time the key to the bottomless pit was available to open it and release further evil developments, the effect of which would darken the minds of men to the enlightenment of Christ's gospel, and the redeeming purposes of God.

9 v. 3-6. And there came out of the smoke locusts upon the earth: and unto them was given power, as the scorpions of the earth have power.

And it was commanded them that they should not hurt the grass of the earth, neither any green thing, neither any tree; but only those men that do not have the seal of God in their foreheads.

And to them it was given that they should not kill them, but that they should be tormented five months: and their torment was the torment of a scorpion, when he striketh a man.

And in those days shall men seek death, and shall not find it; and shall desire to die, and death shall flee from them.

The fifth trumpet or first woe, is in contrast to the first four trumpets that were judgements on the Western third of the Roman Empire that by AD 602 began to be dominated by the Papacy. It was at that time that Mohammed went to his cave to formulate his religion†. We now focus on the Southern or South Eastern parts from Arabia to North Africa, the year AD 612, and the beginning of the Saracen (or Arabian) Empire. The bottomless pit represents the source of these new errors. Mohammed's teaching was accepted in AD 622; that time is known as the Hegira, the first year of the Muslim calendar. These events seem to have given an

---

† *Understanding Islam*. Christian Voice, PO Box 739A, Surbiton, KT6 5YA

incentive to attack that sector of the Roman empire; they erupted with suddenness as a swarm of locusts, for which Rome was unprepared.

Whatever one may think of the teachings of Mohammed, *Revelation* declared these important points; that they would respect trees and growing things because they are part of God's creation, in contrast to the Goths who destroyed anything useful to the Romans, and let it be said to their credit that they allow no idols or images in their worship; and they did not trouble God's sealed ones, who were moving to Britain and all points West, if only because they were not geographically near enough to do so. Their method of conquest was unlike the Romans who killed vast numbers of their enemies; the Saracens preferred to force acceptance of their faith, or the payment of tribute. Many felt this was a fate worse than death.

Five months was allowed for them, (that is, 5 x 30 = 150) days, that on the prophetic scale of a day for a year is 150 years. From AD 612 when Mohammed stirred them into action, it is exactly 150 years until the Caliph made Baghdad his capitol in AD 762. It should be noted that for centuries the River Euphrates was the border between the Roman and Parthian empires so these developments represented a very substantial loss to Rome.

9 v. 7-8. And the shapes of the locusts were like unto horses prepared unto battle; and on their heads were as it were crowns like gold, and their faces were as the faces of men.

And they had hair as the hair of women, and their teeth were as the teeth of lions.

The description is very accurate; they were and still are great horsemen. Their coloured turbans and the long hair with beards are common today.

9 v. 9-10. And they had breastplates, as it were breastplates of iron; and the sound of their wings was as the sound of chariots of many horses running to battle.

And they had tails like unto scorpions, and there were stings in their tails: and their power was to hurt men five months.

The Saracens favoured the use of chain mail for both horse and body armour, which together with long flowing clothes at the gallop made a sound resembling chariots and the flapping of wings. They used the tactics of a cavalry charge, without chariots. The sting in the tail may imply that mounted archers were trained to attack to both the front and rear. The five months being mentioned again may indicate that a second period of 150 years from AD 762 would elapse for their power to decline.

9 v. 11-12. And they had a king over them, which is the angel of the bottomless pit, whose name in the Hebrew tongue is Abaddon, but in the Greek tongue hath his name Apollyon.

One woe is past; and behold, there come two woes more hereafter.

This confirms that the origin and inspiration of Mohammed's faith is not from the Holy Spirit, despite some opinions. It is opposed to the Christian faith. Both names mean the same:- 'Destroyer'. As Jesus explains (*Matthew* 12 v. 26) '*...if Satan cast out Satan...how shall his kingdom stand'*. Here God is allowing one kingdom to oppose and weaken another, so limiting the power of both to oppose His kingdom. At the same time a limit in this case of time is determined, because God in His mercy is not prepared for mankind to embark on a policy of total destruction. That completes the first woe, so we await the sounding of the sixth trumpet heralding the second woe.

9 v. 13-15. And the sixth angel sounded, and I heard a voice from the four horns of the golden altar which is before God,

Saying to the sixth angel which had the trumpet, Loose the four angels which are bound in the great river Euphrates.

And the four angels were loosed, which were prepared for an hour, and a day, and a month, and a year, for to slay the third part of men.

We are now looking at the rise to power of the Turkish Mohammedan Empire. The Turks formerly lived in the Euphrates delta regions, and God has now made them free to move, so in AD 1062 they expanded or overflowed westwards under their leader, Alp Arlsen, into another western section of the Roman Empire. The voice from the altar indicates that this is a further stage of the judgements on Rome. They captured Constantinople, Rome's eastern Capital set up by the Emperor Constantine, and converted the Church of St. Sophia into a mosque, as it remains to this day, but they too were limited in what they were allowed to do by God's time limit of 1 hour + 1 day + 1 month + 1 year. On the year for a day scale that is:-

1/24 year	=	about 2 weeks,
1 day	=	1 year
1 month	=	30 years
1 year	=	360 years
	=	391 years and two weeks.

From (presumably the beginning of May) AD 1062 a further 391 years brings us to their gaining possession of Constantinople on May 16th AD 1453.

At a later point we see the river Euphrates dried up, to indicate their declining power.

9 v. 16-19. And the number of the army of horsemen were two hundred thousand thousand: and I heard the number of them.

And thus I saw the horses in the vision, and them that sat on them, having breastplates of fire, and of jacinth, and brimstone: and the heads of the horses were as the heads of lions: and out of their mouths issued fire and smoke and brimstone.

By these three was the third part of men killed, by the fire, and by the smoke, and by the brimstone, which issued out of their mouths.

For their power is in their mouth, and in their tails: for their tails were like unto serpents, and had heads, and with them they do hurt.

The power of the Turkish Empire was immense, the mind boggles at the resources needed to support an army of millions, and supply all its equipment, that was of the most advanced of its time. The weight of this was directed at the remaining third of the Roman Empire. That is to say after the Goths and Carthaginians had decimated the western sector, and Saracens the southeastern sector. We have before us a detailed description of warfare using firearms. The early cannon were often highly decorated, having muzzles formed as lion's heads, so that the shot, fire and smoke from the gunpowder comes from the mouth. The repeated use of the word 'brimstone' draws our attention to its use as the major epoch making ingredient of gunpowder.

Whereas personal and horse armour was made of iron from earlier dates, it was not possible until the invention of the blast furnace to produce large articles in iron. It is now thought that kings David and Solomon had a primitive blast furnace at Ezion-Geber. The technology for casting bronze into large artefacts is much more ancient, before being used by king Solomon for some temple furniture. Cannon of those days were therefore of bronze and cast into decorative shapes. Their power being in both the mouth and the tail sounds contradictory, but is very significant, for two reasons:

Firstly, the gunpowder is placed first into the cannon (a feature of muzzle loading weapons) and is therefore at its tail being furthest from the mouth, this is the power in the tail to fire the shot. Secondly, the means of transportation was like that used to day by the Royal Horse Artillery on ceremonial occasions, the cannon was horse drawn with the muzzle trailing whilst advancing, thus the power faced backward, but for firing was turned round and the horses removed. Rome's short swords had no chance against this superiority.

This is a very significant part of *Revelation*'s vision; for John not only saw the first use of firearms that have dominated warfare from that time to the present, it was shown to him that sulphur or brimstone was a major ingredient of gunpowder, and also a technical explanation of how the new weapons were transported and worked. Considering that the vision was 1000 years before the event and the limited technical vocabulary available in the first century AD the description is very precise and detailed. John must have struggled to find the words that would convey what he was shown.

9 v. 20- 21 And the rest of the men which were not killed by these plagues yet repented not of the works of their hands, that they should not worship devils, and idols of gold, and silver, and brass, and stone, and of wood: which neither can see, nor hear, nor walk:

Neither repented they of their murders, nor of their sorceries, nor their fornication, nor of their thefts.

Despite these severe losses, and being unable to control the world by force of arms, Rome was unrepentant and determined as ever before to rule the world but by papal power. Total control of the Church and the minds and souls of men was and still is Rome's aim. Their ruthless nature is unchanged from that of former Emperors. Although the Eastern form of Christendom was partly lost to the Turkish Mohammedans, Rome did not stop to take stock of itself and ask, Why did God allow that? It continued in perverting the Faith delivered to us by Christ and the apostles, and made salvation to be as a commercial commodity, and destroyed as many as they could of those who wanted to follow the Apostolic faith.

Chapter 10

10 v. 1- 3.   And I saw another mighty angel come down from heaven, clothed with a cloud: and a rainbow was upon his head, and his face was as it were the sun, and his feet as pillars of fire:

And he had in his hand a little book open; and he set his right foot upon the sea, and his left foot on the earth,

And cried with a loud voice, as when a lion roareth; and when he had cried, seven thunders uttered their voices.

The following are scenes in parenthesis, and may chronologically overlap each other. The seventh trumpet to herald the third woe, is deferred as was the seventh seal, for John and us to see how God is developing His sealed Israel, many of whom are now arrived in the Isles.

This new angel is certainly the Lord Jesus, the description has similarities with that in chapter 1, and He has in His hand the little book that He had previously unsealed and so opened for us. He stands with one foot on the sea, signifying the Isles of the Sea or British Isles, where His people have been gathered into relative security, and the other foot on mainland Europe or Roman earth.
Christ now challenges the powerful but apostate Church of Rome with His revealed truth.

The Reformation had started under the leadership of John Wycliffe (AD 1320-1384), but it was not until the translation of the Bible into English, by William Tyndale, about AD 1526, that it really took off. The arrogant reply from Rome is well described as thunders, for its edicts and bulls were a rejection of God's revealed truth.

10 v. 4-6. And when the seven thunders had uttered their voices, I was about to write: and I heard a voice from heaven saying unto me, Seal up those things which the seven thunders uttered, and write them not.

And the angel which I saw stand upon the sea and upon the earth lifted up his hand to heaven,

And sware by him that liveth for ever and ever, who created heaven, and the things that therein are, and the earth, and the things that

41

therein are, and the sea, and the things which are therein, that there should be time no longer:

The self-righteous attitude of the Roman Church is a fulfilment of prophecy.

When John heard the thunders of the Papacy he was about to record them, but was commanded by the heavenly voice to seal them, and not to write them so that they would not appear as part of God's word. In this way God declares that Rome's threats will not be fully implemented, and their words have no permanence, but will incur further judgements for their defiance.

The declaration of 'time no more', would in modern speech be 'no more time allowed', indication that the next woe or judgement would not be long delayed, to allow further opportunity for Rome to repent: this would otherwise delay God's programme for the further development of His kingdom and people. 'Time no more' does not mean all the clocks stop, although I understand that some believe that God's clock does stop. This in my view indicates that God's clock keeps going to show that one period is drawing to a close so that the next may begin, and at the predetermined set time it will begin.

10 v. 7.   But in the days of the voice of the seventh angel, when he shall begin to sound, the mystery of God should be finished, as he hath declared to his servants the prophets.

This verse is to remind us that although we are still in the period of the sixth trumpet, and the seventh is near, this section is to explain what God is doing to bring blessings unto His people.

10 v. 8-9. And the voice which I heard from heaven spake unto me again, and said, Go and take the little book which is open in the hand of the angel which standeth upon the sea and upon the earth.

And I went unto the angel and said unto him, Give me the little book. And he said unto me, Take it, and eat it up; and it shall make they belly bitter, but it shall be in thy mouth sweet as honey.

John is again told to take an active part in the vision, and to step forward to ask for and receive the little open book. The invitation is to each and every person to come to the Lord and to receive His gospel and word, and he is demonstrating this for us. These actions, first the opening of the sealed book and now the receiving of the opened book, symbolise the Bible being translated into the vernacular, so that it may become available to all. A very great deal of courage and faith is seen in the work of the translators, much of it in the face of opposition and persecution from Rome.

10 v. 10-11. And I took the little book out of the angel's hand, and ate it up; and it was in my mouth sweet as honey: and as soon as I had eaten it, my belly was bitter.

And he said unto me, Thou must prophesy again before many peoples, and nations, and tongues, and kings.

John figuratively eats the book, and here is a sort of play on words, for both the Bible and Christ are referred to as the 'Word'. So there is a parallel between the receiving of the written gospel and receiving Christ as also receiving communion; these are intimately connected, each complementing the other.

The sweetness in the mouth is the good news of the gospel, the forgiveness of sins and the demonstrated love of God by and through the life and atoning work of Christ. On the other hand is the bitterness that followed in the persecutions of those who accepted the plain teaching of scripture, as Rome‡ set about to destroy not only the translators, publishers and the books that were produced, but all those who accepted the pure teaching of the newly revealed word.

The birth of the Reformation was with much pain, but the Holy Spirit was working to bring about a release from the Roman church. The new growth of faith led naturally to accepting responsibility for preaching the word to others, similar to the apostles of the early church. As instructed by the angel, there was seen the need to spread the gospel across the globe.

When considering so great a task as preaching the gospel to a great many nations, the logistics are of utmost importance. There were inspired individuals who just set out to do that, leaving all to follow what to them was a command from the Lord, not waiting for or expecting organised support, their love for Jesus and their fellow men sustained them. There was the need to teach at least basic language skills, and there

‡ Bennett, Richard and de Semlyn, Michael *Papal Rome and the European Union*, Dorchester House Publications, PO Box 67, Rickmansworth, Herts. WD3 5SJ Tel: 01923 286080

was also the need for the Bible or at least parts of it to be translated into a wide range of languages, and the means of producing these in quantity, with other needful supplies and finance.

To do this on the grand scale required the backing and resources of a prosperous nation of an adventurous nature whose economy required expanding markets worldwide. Under the providence of God the people whom He placed in these Isles had the means and were to put their money according to their faith to supporting the ordained witness to nations and kings.

This is not the place for a detailed history of the Reformation. In the turmoil of the time many were unsure what the truth was. It is so now, as we are being conditioned to accept that all faiths or religions are equal and lead us to God: but God wants you to know better.

In *John* 14 v. 6 Jesus said, *'I am the way, the truth, and the life: no man cometh unto the Father but by me'*.

Chapter 11

11 v. 1-2. And there was given me a reed like unto a rod: and the angel stood, saying, Rise, and measure the temple of God, and the altar, and them that worship therein.

But the court which is without the temple leave out, and measure it not; for it is given unto the Gentiles: and the holy city shall they tread under foot forty and two months.

John, in the vision, is given a measuring rod. Older people will remember that a rod, pole or perch, was five and a half yards, a quarter of a chain. For those who now only think metric that is 5.029m. It was a standard formerly in common use. That is not to say that the rod given to John was anything more than symbolic, as it was to be used also to measure the worshippers. All weights and measures are standards that protect the buyer and seller alike from fraudulent practices, and in this case it is to establish the measure of truth that will identify God's Elect and Kingdom, which is the Word of God, the Bible. That is something that can be used to measure the sincerity of the worshippers. We do not have the right to tamper with God's revealed Truth any more than we can choose for ourselves the size of a pint or a metre.

John is told both to measure, and not to measure, as he had previously been told to write, and not to write. He is told to measure the temple, the altar and the worshippers. The temple is the figure of God's dwelling, where He is; The altar represents Christ's perfect sacrifice, once for all and the means of forgiveness of sins to reconcile us to God; the worshippers are the true people of God, those who are at one with God by means of Christ's sacrifice and are by His grace accepting the truth of His Word. These are to be measured by the rod, the standard of truth and righteousness provided by Christ, the angel of the vision.

Outside the temple is the court; the temple had a court for the Gentiles, into which anyone could enter. It seems the nearest to the sanctuary that non-Israelites were permitted, it was for all that, part of the worship area. It was not to be measured because it contained those who would not accept God's revealed Truth, and sought to take over the whole 'temple' with their errors. No falsehood can measure up to God's standard of Truth, and all errors can be identified by it.

We are further informed that they who cannot be measured will control the Holy City which of course includes the temple, the means of salvation and the worshippers. There is only one body ever to achieve this, the Church of Rome, that perverted the pure worship with images and errors. This is permitted by God for a limited period, of forty-two months.

Forty-two months on the day-year prophetic scale is (42 x 30 = 1260 days) = 1260 years, for the Church to be subjected to Rome. Let us look at a few events where the power of the Papacy increased.

a) AD 533 The Bishop of Rome claimed to be head of the universal Church.   + 1260 =   AD 1793
b) AD 596 Austin, later called St Augustine, converted King Ethelbert of Kent.   + 1260 =   AD 1856
c) AD 606 The Decree of Phocas transferred sovereignty to the Pope.   + 1260 =   AD 1866

What happened at the end of 1260 years from each above event that relates to events affecting Israel/Britain, the new homeland of the Ten (or twelve) Tribes, that shows a lessening of Rome's power and influence?

a.   By 1793 both Britain and America were developing Protestant Missionary zeal, and within ten years this was so well organised that The Church Missionary Society and The British and Foreign Bible Society were getting on with taking the gospel of salvation to all the families of the earth, as God had promised Abraham that his seed would do.

b.   1856: the middle of the C19th was marked by a great revival both in Britain and America.

c.   By 1866 the Pope, having long lost sovereignty over England, had by then lost the other European States, and was left with just the Vatican. Severe losses after Rome thought it had all its own way.

11 v. 3-4. And I will give power unto my two witnesses, and they shall prophesy a thousand two hundred and three score days, clothed in sackcloth.

These are the two olive trees, and the two candlesticks standing before the God of the earth.

Notice that we have our 1260 back again, as a period of prophecy or telling forth. Who does God tell us are His witnesses? We have just noted the witness of the Church by its missionary work and spiritual revivals, and to make this quite clear *Revelation* opened with Christ at work among the Church candlesticks (1 v. 13); Who then is the other witness? Is it not the state that was also subjected to Rome during the Dark Ages and threw off that yoke, at the time of Henry VIII and Elizabeth I.

Who then is symbolised by the olive trees? This time we must return to the Old Testament for an answer. In *Zechariah* 4 v. 11-14, we have two olive trees that empty themselves, that is voluntarily give the product of their oil or fruitfulness and pour it through pipes to supply the candlestick which in turn gives light, so that material growth and well being is converted by God's grace into spiritual enlightenment. Notice too, the oil is delivered through pipes so may be in continual use in distant locations if required. And in *Isaiah* 43 v. 10, we have God addressing Jacob/Israel, 'Ye are my witnesses...that ye may know and believe me...' No wonder they were clothed in sackcloth for their testimony was hindered and suppressed by the Papacy throughout the same period known as the Dark Ages.

In the New Testament Paul continues this theme. In *Romans* 11 he likens Israel to an olive tree, from which branches were removed and others grafted in. Teaching us that all who are Christ's have a heritage in the promises to Israel, (but not of course with the Jews until they also accept Christ).

11 v. 5- 6. And if any man will hurt them, fire proceedeth out of their mouth, and devoureth their enemies: and if any man will hurt them, he must in this manner be killed.

These have power to shut heaven that it rain not in the days of their prophecy: and have power over waters to turn them to blood, and to smite the earth with all plagues, as often as they will.

This is God speaking on behalf of His witnesses, as it is not witnesses that judge or determine suitable punishment for a crime, but will have the power to defend themselves. As is normal in our courts the interference with witnesses is a very serious matter, and is dealt with severely. Here God informs those who hurt His witnesses that they will receive His suitable retribution.

11 v. 7-10. And when they shall have finished their testimony, the beast that ascendeth out of the bottomless pit shall make war against them, and shall overcome them, and kill them.

And their dead bodies shall lie in the street of the great city, which spiritually is called Sodom and Egypt, where also our Lord was crucified.

And they of the people and kindreds and tongues and nations shall see their dead bodies three days and an half and shall not suffer their dead bodies to be put in graves.

And they that dwell upon the earth shall rejoice over them, and make merry, and shall send gifts one to another; because these two prophets tormented them that dwelt on the earth.

The Papacy was unable to prevent the translation and enlightening effects of the Bible, it was bitterly opposed to the Reformation, and for a time it seemed that it had been stopped. Daniel in his vision, chapter 7, saw a beast that made war with the saints and overcame them, and changed its form. So with Rome changed from military power to ecclesiastical power. The bodies of the two witnesses lay in the street of the great city, called Sodom and Egypt, (because the burial of heretics was not allowed in consecrated ground.) This is distinct from the beloved or Holy City, but we all know our Lord was not crucified in either Sodom, or in Egypt. Both of those places were punished by God. So why not say Rome when that is the obvious great city. For Jesus died under Rome as did the two witnesses. The reason is simple and we noted it in our introduction: *Revelation* is encoded to prevent the Christians being regarded as enemies of the emperors. The faithful could break the code, and that is what the Reformers did; and they suffered for the exposure of the truth. Rome regarded their death as a reason to celebrate. At the Lateran Council 1516 it was stated, 'There is an end of resistance to Papal rule and religion, nobody opposes any more. (That is from the Lateran Council of 5th May 1514.)

11 v. 11-12. And after three days and an half the Spirit of life from God entered into them, and they stood upon their feet: and great fear fell upon them which saw them.

And they heard a great voice from heaven saying unto them, Come up hither. And they ascended up to heaven in a cloud; and their enemies beheld them.

On 31st October 1517 Martin Luther nailed to the Wittenberg Church door his '95 Theses'. The death of the witnesses was short lived. Rome had lost the battle but never gives up on the war.

11 v. 13- 14. And the same hour was there a great earthquake, and the tenth part of the city fell, and in the earthquake were slain of men seven thousand: and the remnant were affrighted, and gave glory to the God of heaven.

The second woe is past; and, behold, the third woe cometh quickly.

The earthquake was the break away from Rome of the English crown and church, by Henry VIII and Elizabeth I; the seven thousand men are symbolic of the seven Provinces in the Netherlands that followed suit. Others out of fear did the same. These events caused alarm in the Roman earth, it was the culmination of a period of woe and disaster that had lasted from the conquest of Constantinople. This concludes the parenthetical section of where we see God working with His people. Next we will look at the seventh trumpet or third woe.

11 v. 15-17. And the seventh angel sounded; and there were great voices in heaven, saying, The kingdoms of this world are become the kingdoms of our Lord, and of his Christ; and he shall reign forever and ever.

And the four and twenty elders, which sat before God on their seats, fell upon their faces, and worshipped God.

Saying, We give thee thanks, O Lord God Almighty, which art, and wast, and art to come; because thou hast taken to thee thy great power, and hast reigned.

The seventh trumpet signals a further paean of praise in Heaven, for the two witnesses are now active, and being prepared to take the Gospel of Jesus to the world. Israel/Britain began a phenomenal period of expansion both materially and spiritually.

Incidentally the word 'British' means 'Covenant man', and 'Britain' means 'Covenant Land', being a literal translation from Hebrew: and an expression of the promise to David in II *Samuel* 7 v. 10, under the Old

Covenant but now embracing the New. There are similar instances that show up in names that use the consonants B – R – T in that order, for example the Brigantians – BRigan Tians who lived in Northumbria.

11 v. 18. And the nations were angry, and thy wrath is come, and the time of the dead, that they should be judged, and that thou shouldest give reward unto thy servants the prophets, and to the saints, and them that fear thy name, small and great; and shouldest destroy them which destroy the earth.

The time for Divine judgement is approaching, yet despite the evidence of the two witnesses there is no repentance.

11 v. 19. And the temple of God was opened in heaven, and there was seen in his temple the ark of his testament: and there were lightnings, and voices, and thunderings, and an earthquake, and great hail.

Because Revelation is written in a symbolic manner, it should be understood that the 'earth' refers to the Roman dominated region mainly European, or materialistic earth, as distinct from the mainly British with some parts within Europe where God's will was being done, in answer to the prayer 'Thy will be done on earth as it is in heaven' referred to here as 'heaven'. Thus the spiritual dedication that motivated the Reformation with the ark representing Christ's presence, is compared with the dedication of Solomon's temple where the presence of God was visible. In God's programme it was similarly significant.

The symbolic storm represents Rome's opinion of these happy events, and like previous thunders is not recorded in God's word. Likewise it was as an earthquake that shook Rome to its foundations.

You will recall that the seven sealed scroll or book, that the Lamb of God opened for us was written on both sides. This completes the front or first side, so we will now continue with John to share the vision and blessings contained on the reverse side. A sort of new beginning, all the seals are now broken by our Saviour, and we are therefore free to explore, and to receive insight into the fore known plans and purposes of God. We are invited to keep in mind the coded nature of *Revelation*, and to use the scripture's own explanation of its symbols. We need too, to keep in mind that the Judgements of God are primarily for the prevention, curtailing and correction of all sorts of corporate evils, and to bring about opportunities for repentance and reform of systems religious, political, economic or cultural, according to the way that they have impinged on God's Kingdom or holy and beloved city, represented by His two witnesses. This is not the same as for individuals whose status in relation to God's judgements relates to the personal acceptance of Christ and faith in His saving grace, as set out in the gospels and many other scriptures.

Chapter 12

12 v. 1- 2.   And there appeared a great wonder in heaven; a woman clothed with the sun, and the moon under her feet, and upon her head a crown of twelve stars:

and she being with child cried, travailing in birth, and pained to be delivered.

The reverse side of the scroll, or part two of the vision. It opens with the picture of a woman giving birth, whose identity is known from her adornments, a sort of badge of rank. At first sight it may seem to be the Virgin Mary giving birth to Jesus, with king Herod as the dragon, there is an intended parallel as we shall see. The clue to her identity is in *Genesis 37 v. 9.* '… Behold I have dreamed a dream more; and the sun and the moon and the eleven stars made obeisance to me'. Here Joseph is one of the twelve brothers, the twelfth star. This dream was understood by Jacob, to represent himself and his sons. This then shows us that the woman is Jacob/Israel once again depicted in scripture as a woman, descended from the twelve stars, Jacob's sons, in the same manner as in:-

Isaiah 54 v. 5- 6.   For thy Maker is thine husband; the Lord of hosts is his name; and thy Redeemer the Holy One of Israel; The God of the whole earth shall he be called.

For the Lord hath called thee as a woman forsaken and grieved in spirit, and a wife of youth,...

12 v. 3-5. And there appeared another wonder in heaven; and behold a great red dragon, having seven heads and ten horns, and seven crowns upon his heads.

And his tail drew the third part of the stars of heaven, and did cast them to the earth: and the dragon stood before the woman which was ready to be delivered, for to devour her child as soon as it was born.

And she brought forth a man child, who was to rule the nations with a rod of iron: and her child was caught up unto God, and to his throne.

As we saw previously it was Israel in the Isles that gave birth to the Protestant reformed church, and we are reminded of the trauma and pain of that birth. Likewise the birth of Jesus and Herod's action, and the persecution of the early Church that had its birth within Judah/Israel are fitting into this description. We also have to fit this into the right chronology, and it is the dragon's drawing a third of the stars that gives us the clue. As we previously saw that Rome's power base was reduced by the total loss of the eastern and southern sections of the empire, only the western section remaining. This identifies the period as being at least as late as the fall of Constantinople, in 1453, prior to the Reformation.

Thus the dragon failing to destroy Jesus at birth, is shown as having repeated attempts to destroy the true church of Christ. First time, by the Jewish persecution, ended when Titus took Jerusalem and the Jews were dispersed, second, by the Diocletion persecution, that was ended by Constantine a British prince who was proclaimed Emperor at York, and third, by the Papacy, the event referred to in this context, all these were within the Roman sphere of influence. Rome is continuing to work very hard in its objective to bring all the Church under its control at the present time.

The dragon being the enemy of Christ the 'man child' who after His atoning and redeeming work was taken up into heaven, and will rule in righteousness when He returns.

12 v. 6. And the woman fled into the wilderness, where she hath a place prepared of God, that they should feed her there a thousand two hundred and three score days.

This shows us that Israel the woman had passed through and beyond the Roman territory to the appointed place, from being removed from Palestine 1260 days, 1260 years of real time, ending about AD 500, well before the Reformation.

12 v. 7-9. And there was war in heaven: Michael and his angels fought against the dragon: and the dragon fought and his angels.

And prevailed not; neither was their place found any more in heaven.

And the great dragon was cast out, that old serpent, called the Devil and Satan, which deceiveth the whole world: he was cast out into the earth, and his angels were cast out with him.

The implications of these verses are profound. We are being told that there is a great spiritual war going on. Jesus said, '*I behold Satan as lightning fall from heaven*', (*Luke* 10 v. 18). Being in rebellion against

God he is banished to earth, and here continues his attempts to destroy all who truly seek to serve God and follow Jesus. We are also informed, *'And at that time shall Michael stand up, the great prince that standeth for the children of thy people: and there shall be a time of trouble, such as never was since there was a nation even to that same time: and at that time thy people shall be delivered, every one that shall be found written in the book'*, (*Daniel* 12 v. 1). From this we see that Michael has a substantial role in protecting Israel from satanic attacks, probably mainly at the spirit level, to frustrate attempts to destroy both Israel and the faith in Jesus. This conflict is shown as becoming progressively more severe as it spills over into the material, and manifests itself in the wars between Israel/Britain and various countries of Europe. Since Satan can no longer oppose God in heaven, he targets Israel and the reformed church that God holds dear and however unworthy is determined to use for His glory. There are several occasions when the angelic forces have been seen and intervened to aid us in the arena of conflict. (*The White Cavalry* and *Angels of Mons*).

If the whole world is deceived, we have grounds for saying that what is generally accepted may well be wrong, and should come under scrutiny.

12 v. 10-11. And I heard a loud voice saying in heaven, Now is come salvation, and strength, and the kingdom of our God, and the power of his Christ: for the accuser of our brethren is cast down, which accused them before God day and night.

And they overcame him by the blood of the Lamb, and the word of their testimony; and they loved not their lives unto death.

There is a proclamation in heaven announcing a further stage of the establishment of God's kingdom on earth as the power of Rome was repelled and failed to prevent the establishment of the reformed faith and sovereignty in Britain, albeit at the price paid by many martyrs. The two witnesses of church and state under the crown, stand together.

12 v. 12-14. Therefore rejoice, ye heavens, and ye that dwell in them. Woe to the inhabiters of the earth and of the sea! For the devil is come down unto you, having great wrath, because he knoweth that he hath but a short time.

And when the dragon saw that he was cast unto the earth, he persecuted the woman, which brought forth the man child.

And to the woman were given two wings of a great eagle, that she might fly into the wilderness, into her place, where she is nourished for a time, and times, and half a time, from the face of the serpent.

We were moments ago looking at events from a mainly spiritual viewpoint, here I think we see the same things from a mainly material view. There is rejoicing in heaven that God's word is opened and translated for all, and the reformed church and sovereignty is re-established, this had its manifestation within Israel/Britain, also called heaven when God is honoured, where there was immense popular support fro these developments, in spite of some Royal excesses, that led to serious civil strife. This also caused distress to the papal infallibility, whose authority throughout Europe, the Roman earth, was badly dented. There is a play on words, for as Satan was cast out of heaven, the papal repulsion from Israel/Britain, is seen as a parallel material re-enactment. In order to recoup its losses the dragon embarks on a programme of persecutions, spiritually to pervert the reformed faith, and also by military and naval actions.

By God's grace these attempts failed, and the Divine purpose was advanced, and cannot fail provided the reformed faith is adhered to; but the dragon sees no price in blood too high to pay. We have our old friend 1260 years again, $(360 + 2 \times 360 + \frac{1}{2} \times 360)$. Note that by adding the two periods together, we have 2520 years = the 7 times of punishment or retraining = 7×360 years.

You have most likely noticed that throughout *Revelation* there is a sort of duality, where the forces of good and evil are shown as opposing each other, but also the message is divided unto earthly and heavenly viewpoints and in this case time is also divided. Philosophically good and evil are assumed to be equal and opposite, but nowhere in the Bible is this view supported. The material world is controlled by time, there are physical limits to everything in our experience; but the spiritual forces that are the motivation for material actions are not limited by time in the sense that we understand it, but can operate in or across any material time periods. *Revelation's* message is absolutely clear, that in the end Our Lord Jesus Christ will have the final word and bring all things under His rule of perfect peace, and harmony with Himself, and restore all to perfection. Until then the conflict will continue in any form.

This second period of 1260 years is clearly stated as the Israel woman being nourished in her own place. This period began badly with the British Church being perverted by Rome in the person of Augustine, and papal power over the monarchy and church until the Reformation. The symbolic wings represent transportation to the promised homelands, where the Channel and oceans have been a partial defence against the dragon's assaults. During this partial respite Israel/Britain has had much growth in numbers, power, territories, and spiritual maturity, to the dragon's extreme displeasure. We are told that the devil knows his time is nearly up, so, at the end of that period he has increased his efforts to deceive and destroy. Force of arms has failed every time, by the grace of God. Now as time for Christ to return draws near, urgency makes events move faster and new weapons are being used. These include a range of measures introduced to diminish the authority of God's Word, like higher criticism, the evolutionary theories, down grading of Sunday from a rest and worship day, political correctness, the abandonment of Christian education in many schools, the social gospel adopted in many churches, and the notion that Britain cannot survive without being controlled by Europe, are just a few. These things have been introduced gradually and over a number of years so that few will notice and less will object. Now we have reached the point where it is impossible to reverse the process, or so we are being led to believe. On the other hand the Almighty takes a very different stand.

Isaiah 54 v. 17. No weapon that is formed against thee shall prosper; and every tongue that shall rise against thee in judgment thou shalt condemn. This is the heritage of the servants of the LORD, and their righteousness is of me, saith the LORD.

This is very reassuring, but, remember the benefits of the promises are to the faithful, and we may ask ourselves, 'Why should God protect those who reject Him'? Mercifully God remains concerned and intervenes to implement His covenanted obligations, and to bring about circumstances that are corrective.

12 v. 15-17. And the serpent cast out of his mouth water as a flood after the woman, that he might cause her to be carried away of the flood.

And the earth helped the woman, and the earth opened her mouth, and swallowed up the flood which the dragon cast out of his mouth.

And the dragon was wroth with the woman, and went to make war with the remnant of her seed, which keep the commandments of God, and have the testimony of Jesus Christ.

Sometimes the wisdom of the wise is hard to follow – this last verse in Schofield References edition is subtitled 'The Jewish Remnant'. We know that the Jews try to keep the commandments of God, but where is their testimony of Jesus Christ? Until they accept the testimony of Jesus that cannot be correct. We need to be very careful when handling God's Word for it is so easy to fall flat on our faces, by jumping to the wrong conclusion.

This has rightly been attributed to the flood of fierce opposition to the Reformation that was directed in particular against England, and its Protestant monarchy. The European or Roman earth helped our cause at that time as Protestantism became popular in parts of Europe as the continental Reformation was led by Martin Luther, thus taking some of the force away from Britain and fulfilling this section of the prophecy. There is a more up to date aspect of this, as under the many ramifications of the Treaty of Rome, intended to ensnare Britain, the European nations have also helped to thwart the Dragon's plans as they disagree and their corruption becomes common knowledge. At the moment of preparing this British politics is preparing for a Parliamentary election campaign, and there is a damming report on electoral fraud concerning postal voting in local elections at Birmingham; the Judge said, it would disgrace a banana republic. Preparations are being made for the funeral of Pope John Paul II, so Charles and Camilla have to rearrange their wedding day. The news is like a Gilbertian script. No doubt there will soon be new directions as a result of all these things.

It is a remarkable fact that the Roman Church has to elect a new leader from time to time: but the Protestant churches never have to do that as their leader is alive for ever. Alleluia!

Be assured the dragon will soon make renewed attempts to bring the Protestant churches under the Roman umbrella.

Chapter 13

13 v. 1- 2.   And I stood upon the sand of the sea, and saw a beast rise up out of the sea, having seven heads and ten horns, and upon his horns ten crowns, and upon his heads the name of blasphemy.

And the beast which I saw was like unto a leopard, and his feet were as the feet of a bear, and his mouth as the mouth of a lion: and the dragon gave him his power, and his seat, and great authority.

Another change of scenery. The sand of the sea is a symbol of the seed of Abraham (*Genesis* 32 v. 12) and confirms that they are at that time become very numerous. Thus the viewpoint of this section is from Israel's new homeland which has the Church within it. We see a blasphemous fabulous beast rise from the sea, that is, the nations (of Europe). The variety of the parts of this beast indicates that it is the product or inheritor of the former empires from Babylon to Rome. The seven heads tell us that Rome has had various forms of government. When John recorded this vision it was the time of the Imperial Caesars, the sixth form. The dragon gives his powers to this new beast. This shows the transition to the seventh form being the Papacy, and because the origins go back to Babylon, and Nebuchadnezzar's dream, it is sometimes in this and other prophecies referred to as 'Babylon'.

13 v. 3-4. And I saw one of his heads as it were wounded to death; and his deadly wound was healed: and all the world wondered at the beast.

And they worshipped the dragon which gave power to beast: and they worshipped the beast, saying,

Who is like unto the beast? Who is able to make war with him?

This last is the head having the seemingly fatal wound. At the Reformation the credibility of the papacy was destroyed, the errors of its religious system were exposed. The world might wonder how it could survive after such a blow as the loss of the English Church, and other losses on the continent. But the papacy has all the powers of its predecessors, and set about recovering its losses. The prophetical earth, Europe for the most part, still believed in the Papacy and its supposed invincibility. Only the Risen Lord Jesus, the Almighty Son of God has the power to deal with this beast, but it pleases Him to involve and share now His sufferings with His redeemed Israel, and His true church, as His witnesses in the struggle, and then, He will share with them the ultimate victory.

13 v. 5-6. And there was given unto him a mouth speaking great things and blasphemies; and power was given unto him to continue forty and two months.

And he opened his mouth in blasphemy against God, to blaspheme his name, and his tabernacle, and them that dwell in heaven.

We have seen the forty-two months in chapter 11, which ended in AD 1866 when Victor Emmanuel was made king of Italy, and the popes were no longer kings of kings. The blasphemies are not only the idolatry such as worshipping Mary as the Mother of God, but the arrogance of claiming the power of life and death over any opposition, committing thousands of acts of brutality, in God's name.

The tabernacle represents the Reformed Church wherein we have seen the Christ, and heaven is a symbolic name for Israel/Britain, where and when they were at least attempting to do God's Will 'on earth as it is in heaven'. Rome set about destabilising the Reformed Church, the nation and throne by force of arms, plots (as the Gunpowder plot) and subterfuges.

13 v. 7-10. And it was given unto him to make war with the saints, and to overcome them: and power was given him over all kindreds, and tongues, and nations.

And all that dwell upon the earth shall worship him, whose names are not written in the book of life of the Lamb slain from the foundation of the world.

If any man have an ear, let him hear.

He that leadeth into captivity shall go into captivity: he that killeth with the sword must be killed with the sword. Here is the patience and the faith of the saints.

The saints, not Matthew, Mark, etc., or those that have been canonised, but simply the true followers of Jesus, against whom we saw Rome was opposed. This is a warning that Rome will continue its opposition to Christ's church and nation by some means or power, and will overcome them. This implies that the true church and nation, the two witnesses will again seem to be lost, and all will worship in the manner determined by the Roman church; except those who are not deceived because their names are already in the Lamb's book of life. Will this be something like Christ on the cross, when it appeared that his mission had ended in tragedy? Again we see that He allows His followers to share His suffering, so that he can share with them His great victory.

This would mean hard decisions for modern Christians to make --- but due to the inroads that Roman Catholic sympathisers have made into Protestant theological institutions, prophecy and its interpretation is rarely taught. Therefore most spiritual leaders do not touch the message of *Revelation* or the other prophetic books; so their flocks are ignorant of Christ's message and warnings and think that talk of church unity is the only way forward. *Revelation* shows us that there will be suitable judgements against the deceivers.

13 v. 11-12. And I beheld another beast coming up out of the earth; and he had two horns like a lamb, and he spoke like a dragon.

And he exerciseth all the power of the first beast before him, and causeth the earth and them that dwell therein to worship the first beast, whose deadly wound was healed.

John is being shown for our benefit, another form, or change in the tactics of the dragon – beast – papal initiative. There will be a new means of causing all to submit to papal authority and doctrine.

13 v.13-15. And he doeth great wonders, so that he maketh fire come down from heaven on the earth in the sight of men,

And deceiveth them that dwell on the earth by the means of those miracles which he had power to do in the sight of the beast; saying to them that dwell on the earth, that they should make an image to the beast, which had the wound by a sword, and did live. And he had power to give life unto the image of the beast, that the image of the beast should both speak, and cause that as many as would not worship the image of the beast should be killed.

Jesus is plainly telling us that this is a deception. But what sort? It is not God's fire from heaven, but their own that they want you to believe is of God. This is not a literal statue or idol, it is a symbol representing a body or instrument set up to perform the papacy's will. The Lateran Councils were just that. They were used to discipline and destroy with appalling cruelty. At the Council of Constance in 1416, Huss and Jerome were deemed to be heretics, and condemned to be burned at the stake, claiming this to be the just judgement of God! The Lateran Councils were but the first of a line, in more modern times we have the Treaty of Rome and the Council of Ministers that have been proven to be corrupt. Surprise, surprise! Is this the new secret weapon, - or, is there to be yet another? Let us not speculate, but remain watchful.

13 v. 16-18. And he causeth all, both small and great, rich and poor, free and bond, to receive a mark in their right hand, or in their foreheads:

And that no man might buy or sell, save that he had the mark, or the name of the beast, or the number of his name.

Here is wisdom. Let him that hath understanding count the number of the beast: for it is the number of a man; and his number is Six hundred three score and six.

Marks of this sort in John's day were used on slaves, and implied that those so marked were subject to their owner's undisputed power.

The Lateran Councils denied trade with heretics, and their burial in consecrated ground.

The ramifications of the Treaty of Rome, control all trade. This is done by the VAT, where traders of all kinds are required to have a number and use it on all business documents.

The number on the right hand represents the writing of all invoices etc., and the number on the forehead is the VAT registered number on the billheads and letterheads of all businesses. Serious troubles await those who do not conform. We have become slaves to this system.

St. Paul had these times in mind when he wrote to the Thessalonians, as we shall see in a few moments.

In Greek, and Hebrew, letters of the alphabet have numeric value. If in any word the numeric values of the letters are added together a numeric value for that word is found. The numeric value of some words have interesting common factors, for example:-

MAN = 666(6x3x37) GOD = 35 (7x5)

JESUS = 888 (8x3x37) CHRIST = 1480 (8x5x37)

II Thessalonians 2 v.1-12. Now we beseech you, brethren, by the coming of our Lord Jesus Christ, and by our gathering together unto him,

That ye be not soon shaken in mind or be troubled, neither by spirit, nor by word, nor by letter as from us, as that the day of Christ is at hand.

Let no man deceive you by any means: for that day shall not come, except there come a falling away first, and that man of sin be revealed, the son of perdition;

Who opposeth and exalteth himself above all that is called God, or that is worshipped; so that he as God sitteth in the temple of God, shewing himself that he is God.

Remember ye not, that, when I was yet with you, I told these things?

And now ye know what withholdeth that he might be revealed in his time.

For the mystery of iniquity doth already work: only he who now letteth will let, until he be taken out of the way.

And then shall that Wicked be revealed, whom the Lord shall consume with the spirit of his mouth, and shall destroy with the brightness of his coming:

Even him, whose coming is after the working of Satan with all power and signs and lying wonders,

And with all deceivableness of unrighteousness in them that perish; because they received not the love of the truth, that they might be saved.

And for this cause God shall send them strong delusion, that they should believe a lie:

That they all might be damned who believed not the truth, but had pleasure in unrighteousness.

Chapter 14

14 v. 1- 3.   And I looked, and lo, a Lamb stood on the mount Sion, and with him an hundred forty and four thousand, having his Father's name written on their foreheads.

And I heard a voice from heaven as the sound of many waters, and as the voice of a great thunder: and I heard the voice of harpers harping with their harps:

And they sung as it were a new song before the throne, and before the four beasts, and the elders: and no man could learn that song but the hundred and forty and four thousand, which were redeemed from the earth.

Sion is a name originally for the top of Mount Hermon, but the Israelities used it as an additional name for the south west of Jerusalem, David's citadel or Zion, implying that it was holy and where God was to be found. The mentions of it in the New Testament convey this latter connection, as in:-

Hebrews 12 v. 22- 24.   But ye are come unto mount Sion, and unto the city of the living God, the heavenly Jerusalem, and to an innumerable company of angels,

To the general assembly and church of the firstborn, which are written in heaven, and to God the Judge of all, and to the spirits of just men made perfect,

And to Jesus the mediator of the new covenant, and the blood of sprinkling, that speaketh better things than that of Abel.

So if you are at Sion you are found to be with God and all those witnesses, as the hundred and forty four thousand whom we saw in chapter 7 were the redeemed and sealed from all the Tribes of Israel. We use seals to show ownership or security as on a legal document, or the electric company puts a seal on the meter to ensure that it is not tampered with. These people are not slaves as we saw previously that were marked to ensure that they worshipped the beast. These are God's freemen, freed from the power of sin by the Redeemer's blood, and it is His mark of His blood that they bear.

This is cause enough for a further paean of praise in the heavenly realm, as Jesus is seen among His people. Remember John is seeing things in heaven and on earth at the same time, because he described heaven as having a glass like floor; what he sees in heaven is also seen as describing events on earth. As Israel heard the voice of God at Sinai as if it thundered, so again God's voice is heard, this time the thunder is the power of God's written word, as will be seen in a few moments. It caused them to sing a new song, of glory to God and of sins forgiven; the opposite to the record of those going into captivity where they refused to sing the songs of Zion in Babylon, and hung up their harps. (*Psalm* 137). The new songs, of the Reformation, could be sung in the new homeland, a symbolic heaven on earth, that God had led his sealed ones to, and only they wherever they were had the ability to learn it.

14 v. 4-5. These are they which were not defiled with women; for they are virgins. These are they which follow the Lamb whithersoever he goeth. These were redeemed from among men, being the first fruits unto God and to the Lamb.

And in their mouth was found no guile: for they are without fault before the throne of God.

Quite obviously not all the Reformed Church or the nation are virgins, it symbolically tells us that their form of worship and national administration had a purity pleasing to God. Only the papacy finds fault.

14 v. 6-7. And I saw another angel fly in the midst of heaven, having the everlasting gospel to preach unto them that dwell on the earth, and to every nation, and kindred, and tongue, and people.

Saying with a loud voice, Fear God, and give glory to him; for the hour of his judgement is come: and worship him that made heaven, and earth, and the sea, and the fountains of waters.

We had seen previously that Israel/Britain had become numerous, materially prosperous and spiritually mature. The necessary prerequisites to undertake on a large scale a work for God's glory. Here we see another angel, or messenger, in the midst of heaven having the everlasting gospel-; heaven we had also noticed is sometimes symbolically used to denote the place of Israel/Britain, where the Reformed church was, and God's will was done as in heaven. This shows us that this is where preparations were under way to launch a great missionary campaign in many languages to many countries, worldwide. The expansion of world trade and colonisation were the vehicle for spreading and supporting the missionary work, and the vast task of translating, publishing and distribution of God's word into just about every known tongue is still ongoing. The nations have been given the gospel, the good news that Jesus forgives sins, the way to avoid God's judgements on wilful unbelievers. But it is still their choice; and they have been warned.

14 v. 8.   And there followed another angel, saying, Babylon is fallen, is fallen, that great city, because she made all nations drink of the wine of the wrath of her fornication.

This angel declares the collapse of the Babylonian system and sequence of empires up to the Roman systems of the present time, as outlined in Nebuchadnezzar's dream. (*Daniel* 2).

14 v. 9-11. And the third angel followed them, saying with a loud voice, If any man worship the beast and his image, and receive his mark in his forehead, or in his hand,

The same shall drink of the wine of the wrath of God, which is poured out without mixture into the cup of his indignation; and he shall be tormented with fire and brimstone in the presence of the holy angels, and in the presence of the Lamb:

And the smoke of their torment ascendeth up forever and ever: and they have no rest day nor night, who worship the beast and his image, and whosoever receiveth the mark of his name.

A further warning to all who support the beasts' Roman system, they will receive the full force of God's indignation, a horrifying prospect. In chapter 9 we saw brimstone used in gunpowder against Rome for the first time, this may indicate great hostilities without mercy, perhaps with advanced weaponry, but it could also remind us of the destruction of Sodom and the cities nearby, where to this day are found lumps of brimstone and evidence of fierce burning and great disaster. As this occurs in the presence of angels and Christ the Lamb, the latter may seem to be more probable. Whatever it may be the evidence of it will remain for a very long time. Later we shall see destruction in one day and one hour, so this event may be a final chastisement intended to give a final opportunity for repentance by those seduced into supporting the beast. If so, it show God's extreme reluctance to withdraw his mercy. It may explain, or be the cause of events at the end of chapter 17, where we shall see followers of the beast system change sides and taking revenge.

14 v. 12-13. Here is the patience of the saints: here are they that keep the commandments of God, and the faith of Jesus.

And I heard a voice from heaven saying unto me, Write, Blessed are the dead which die in the Lord from henceforth: Yea, saith the Spirit, that they may rest from their labours; and their works do follow them.

Here is encouragement for those who may die in conflict, or witness and defence of church and state, the two witnesses, for they will rest, but their work for the Lord will continue or follow after them, and they, will be raised to continue their service to the Lord. In *Ezekiel* 37 we are told that all Israel shall be raised as a great army, many may not deserve it, but God always gives us better than we deserve.

14 v. 14-16. And I looked, and behold a white cloud, and upon the cloud one sat like unto the Son of man, having on his head a golden crown, and in his hand a sharp sickle.

And another angel came out of the temple, crying with a loud voice to him that sat on the cloud, Thrust in thy sickle, and reap: for the time is come for thee to reap; for the harvest of the earth is ripe.

And he that sat on the cloud thrust in his sickle on the earth; and the earth was reaped.

The scene changes again. In chapter 10 Christ was clothed in a cloud to give the little book to John; here He is on a cloud, carrying a sickle, as was commonly used before the age of mechanisation for reaping. This is the time for the reaping of the earth, of which Jesus spoke in his parable of the wheat and tares. (*Matthew* 13 v. 24-30). The tares were introduced by stealth, and represent false teachings and ideologies that cannot be removed until maturity, as only then are they reliably recognised, collected and burned. This must take place first, after which the wheat will be gathered, representing the children of His Kingdom.

We have here a representation of the commencement of an horrific event, here Christ is seen to be about to act in judgement on all who have opposed Him, and have caused the suffering of His followers and witnesses.

14 v. 17-18. And another angel came out of the temple which is in heaven, he also having a sharp sickle. And another angel came out from the altar, which had power over fire; and he cried with a loud cry to him that had the sharp sickle, saying, Thrust in thy sharp sickle, and gather the clusters of the vine of the earth; for her grapes are fully ripe.

The time for the harvest of the vine of the earth is announced. This is similar to Joel's vision.

Joel 3 v. 13 & 16. Put ye in the sickle, for the harvest is ripe: come, get you down; for the press is full, the fats overflow; for their wickedness is great...The Lord also shall roar out of Zion, and utter his voice from Jerusalem; and the heavens and the earth shall shake: but the Lord will be the hope of his people, and the strength of the children of Israel.

The mention of Jerusalem and Zion, in the context of *Revelation* would show the involvement of Israel/Britain in this event, the Lord being our hope and strength. What a mercy!

14 v. 19-20. And the angel thrust in his sickle into the earth, and gathered the vine of the earth, and cast it into the great winepress of the wrath of God.

And the winepress was trodden without the city, and blood came out of the winepress, even unto the horse bridles, by the space of a thousand and six hundred furlongs.

Conflict, with loss of life on a horrendous scale is described here. But when? What past events could this be referring to? Perhaps World Wars I & II are within this description. If so, the process has started, or is completed. The reference to the sickle may be to the emblem of Russia, and shows the communist revolutions in predominantly Roman Catholic countries of Europe, and much loss of influence and power to the Papacy.

There seem to be at least three aspects to this:-

First, aggression by the Axis powers that were severely weakened by an untimely conflict with Russia. *(Hammer and Sickle)*.

Second, the overrunning of countries by Communism. *(Hammer and Sickle)*.

67

Third, a new act of aggression by Russia against European countries, the place where the vine of the earth grows, as distinct from the true vine of Christ; following the introduction of formerly Communist countries into the papal homeland of Western Europe's European Community. Possibly as a diversion to a move on Palestine and Middle East oil, that other prophets indicate. Such a strategy would throw the 'West' into disarray and reduce the prospect of opposition to obtaining the greater prize of oil that would then be denied to the West. *(Hammer and Sickle).*

The phrase 'without the city' has at least three or four separate and compatible meanings:-

a) It could mean 'the great city', symbolic Babylon, the Roman earth in general, as when the European armies had gone to Russia, and were beaten more by the natural forces of the weather than the Russians, outside of their own territory.

b) It could mean outside Rome the centre of papal power, not itself devastated as some German and British cities in WWII.

c) The 1600 furlongs, or two hundred miles with no major city, is a fair estimate of the beaches invaded on 'D' day, which is regarded as a turning point in WWII.

d) Or it could mean the holy city in the prophetic sense Israel Britain, the territory of the two witnesses that the Axis powers were unable to invade and subdue, despite careful planning.

None should be complacent just because God gave us victory at that time, if Britain continues to flirt with Rome further suffering is bound to follow. We shall be suitably disciplined for our folly, unless a state of repentance is reached. The warnings are there and very clear!

In any case the distance of 1,600 furlongs, makes this an event too large to take place entirely very near any known city, unless largely surrounding it, and not involving the inside, it most probably describes an event in open country.

As we continue into chapter 15, we are coming to the end of a series of scenes concerning Israel/Britain which as history developed included the Commonwealth and the United States, and contrasting these with papal and European Powers and others.

Chapter 15

15 v.1. And I saw another sign in heaven, great and marvellous, seven angels having the seven last plagues; for in them is filled up the wrath of God.

We watch as John in the spirit stands in heaven near God's throne, these angels have with them vials of the last plagues of the wrath of God. Highly dangerous and destructive contents: visualise the hazard warnings on them. HANDLE WITH EXTREME CARE. USE ONLY AS INSTRUCTED BY SUPREME AUTHORITY. These angels being called into this position must rank among the most ominous scenes in all the Bible.

15 v. 2-3. And I saw as it were a sea of glass mingled with fire: and them that had gotten the victory over the beast, and over his image, and over his mark, and over the number of his name, stand on the sea of glass, having the harps of God.

And they sing the song of Moses the servant of God, and the song of the Lamb, saying, Great and marvellous are thy works, Lord God Almighty; just and true are thy ways, thou King of saints.

Here is seen the release of the Israel nations from the power of the Papacy shown as the beast and its oppressive power. Described as being like the release from Pharaoh's power when God drowned his army in the Red sea, about which Moses and the people sang. (*Exodus* 15). This was an unexpected defeat, just when Pharaoh thought he had them totally in his power. This may, by mentioning Moses, indicate that the demise of papal and European power will be by some unexpected and sudden cause: if we do not have that method revealed to us, we will not be able spoil the surprise.

15 v. 4-5. Who shall not fear thee, O Lord, and glorify thy name? For thou only art holy: for all nations shall come and worship before thee; for thy judgements are made manifest.

And after that I looked, and, behold, the temple of the tabernacle of the testimony in heaven was opened:

It is here further emphasised that the forthcoming judgements of God are corrective in purpose to bring all nations to the point of worshipping only Him, instead of the beast, or any other gods.

The opening of the tabernacle of testimony, shows God's point of jurisdiction and justice is revealed as the centre of Christ's command, in readiness for the ordering of the first resurrection and the coming plagues.

15 v. 6-7. And the seven angels came out of the temple, having the seven plagues, clothed in pure and white linen, and having their breasts girded with golden girdles.

And one of the four beasts gave unto the seven angels seven golden vials full of the wrath of God, who liveth forever and ever.

Although these angels have what we may well think of as very distasteful duties to perform, we should notice that in their dress they emulate their, and our Master, by wearing the golden girdles over their hearts: as Jesus did in chapter 1. This shows that it is out of love for creation as a whole that these measures need to be taken, as a step towards the coming rule of Christ.

So important is this scene that we have been introduced to it in stages. First we are introduced to the idea of seven vials of God's wrath handed to them. The stage as John sees it is set, and the situation on earth is to follow the pattern seen by him in heaven. They must now wait for the command to pour them out.

15 v. 8.   And the temple was filled with smoke from the glory of God, and from his power; and no man was able to enter into the temple, till the seven plagues of the seven angels were fulfilled.

Because the judgements of God are in progress, no one enters the temple or the presence of His overwhelming power. No one, no politician, no president, has the power to thwart His purpose. He may use them and set one against another to break their power. This is the Almighty having the last word. He will use the power that He allows these people to have in His own way. When the coming turmoil of this age ends Christ will be supreme, and will rule with those whose names are written in His Book of Life because they dedicated their lives to His service, and He will give them a role in His Kingdom. This is the last and final warning of the seventh trumpet or third woe that has been deferred from Chapter 11, while we were shown other scenes and explanations, as God's plans were revealed.

Chapter 16

16 v. 1. And I heard a great voice out of the temple saying to the seven angels, Go your ways, and pour out the vials of the wrath of God upon the earth.

The command of God is given for His judgements to proceed. This is not the last judgement, but that of the earth in the prophetic sense of the European nations controlled by the beast, and the Papal system including its Middle Eastern Allies. We will see judgements on the earth, the sea, the rivers, the sun, the seat of the beast, the Euphrates and the air: in a similar manner to the trumpets in chapters 8 and 9.

Some are going to wonder why it is that God is so wrathful against these powers, and not against say China or India for their strange religions. There is a simple answer, only the Roman and Muslim orientated powers have opposed God's Witnesses, and sought to destroy the true worship and faith as revealed in the Bible. These other powers and religions have not attempted to do that, if only because they have not been geographically in a position to try. God is not punishing or disciplining people for what they did not attempt do.

16 v. 2. And the first went, and poured out his vial upon the earth; and there fell a noisome and grievous sore upon the men who had the mark of the beast, and upon them that worshipped his image.

This represents the French Revolution of 1789, by 1793 the masses turned against the aristocracy. This appalling bloodshed left a power vacuum that led later to the rise of Napoleon. This revolution had knock-on effects in other European countries, so that much of Europe was plunged into chaos.

On the other hand Israel/Britain had instead a religious revival, without which it may well have suffered a revolution also, so spiritually speaking Israel Britain was in opposition to the kind of remedy for its ills that overtook France, we had instead a spiritual revolution.

16 v. 3. And the second angel poured out his vial upon the sea; and it became as the blood of a dead man: and every living soul died in the sea.

Poured out on the sea, this is referring to sea power and naval actions. Here again Israel Britain, God's servant nation, is being used to act for Him against the beast powers. The French and Spanish sea power was destroyed between 1793 and 1805 in battles as at Toulon, Ushant, Cape St. Vincent, the Nile and Trafalgar.

16 v. 4-7. And the third angel poured out his vial upon the rivers and fountains of waters; And they became blood.

And I heard the angel of the waters say, Thou art righteous, O Lord, which art, and wast, and shalt be, because thou hast judged thus.

For they have shed the blood of saints and prophets, and thou hast given them blood to drink; for they are worthy.

And I heard another out of the altar say, Even so, Lord God Almighty, true and righteous are thy judgements.

God remembers the vast numbers of martyrs of Europe, Lutherans, Hussites, Waldenses, Huguenots, and others who held to their faith in Jesus, and would not bow down to the beast. The French invasion of its European neighbours, led by Napoleon, devastated the regions of the rivers Danube, Poe, and Rhine, among whose valleys so many martyrs had died.

The angel of the waters confirms that this was the right place for this judgement to fall.

The other voice from the altar, the place of sacrifice, is in response to chapter 6 v. 10, 'How long, O Lord, holy and true, dost thou not judge and avenge our blood on them that dwell on the earth?' The martyrs also confirm this is a deferred just judgement.

16 v. 8-9. And the fourth angel poured out his vial upon the sun; and power was given unto him to scorch men with fire.

And men were scorched with great heat, and blasphemed the name of God, which hath power over these plagues: and they repented not to give him glory.

The symbol of the sun is used to indicate the most prominent ruler of the time, in this case Napoleon, and during his reign atheism thrived. He had no respect for the papal system, or any of the papal monarchies: by his exploit they were removed. He was pleased to have the Pope for his coronation, but quickly forgot his loyalty to the same and sort of bit the hand that helped him. Even Italy rejected papal sovereignty, and the Napoleonic Wars 1866-1870 caused severe losses to the papacy. Despite these losses there was no hint of repentance from Rome: if there had been, God would have forgiven them as it says in *Jeremiah* 51 v 9. '*We would have healed Babylon....*'

16 v. 10-11. And the fifth angel poured out his vial upon the seat of the beast; and his kingdom was full of darkness; and they gnawed their tongues for pain,

And blasphemed the God of heaven because of their pains and their sores, and repented not of their deeds.

Vial 5 concerns much the same period as vial 4. This concerns specifically the throne or seat of the papacy, at the time when the Pope was exiled from Rome. After Garibaldi's campaign and Victor Emmanuel was crowned king in 1870, the popes were allowed back but were confined to the Vatican City. Considering that the popes regarded all Europe and beyond as their property that was quite some come down by any standard, no wonder his kingdom was full of darkness. Even that humiliation produced only blasphemies and no repentance.

16 v. 12. And the sixth angel poured out his vial upon the great river Euphrates; and the water thereof was dried up, that the way of the kings of the east might be prepared.

We noticed the parallels between the trumpets and the vials. The sixth both refer to the Turkish power. The trumpet indicated the rise of the Turkish Empire, thus the vial shows its demise or drying up. Russia had developed aspirations to control the Middle East, at least to obtain warm water Black Sea ports, hence the Russian-Turkish wars.

a) This seems to indicate that Russia, an amalgam of several Socialist Republics, is here called the 'kings of the east'. Russian Communism spread to the Roman Catholic countries of Europe following the First World War, to the further distress of the papacy. In WWI Turkey was allied to Germany, so that the British Empire was fighting on two fronts, Europe and Palestine. The collapse of the Turks at Jerusalem tended to shorten that war.

b) At the same time God had other plans to advance. Because of rebellion against God, all the tribes of Israel went into captivity. BC

603 saw the Jews removed to Babylon, some went back to Jerusalem assisted by the Decree of Cyrus, but never gained full independence, even at the time of Christ they were at best a province of the Roman Empire who later re-dispersed them. The period of exile for Israel was to be 2520 years, this expired in 1917 as the Turks left the Holy City, and General Allenby received the Keys shown on the cover of this book as tokens of surrender§, without a shot being fired. Thus the period of Gentile domination of the Holy City ended when it passed into the hands of Israel/Britain. The fact that Palestine is no longer under British control does not invalidate the fulfilment of the exile period. It did prepare the way for the Jews to go to Palestine that began under British Mandate.

16 v. 13-16. And I saw three unclean spirits like frogs come out of the mouth of the dragon, and out of the mouth of the beast, and out of the mouth of the false prophet.

For they are the spirits of devils, working miracles, which go forth unto the kings of the earth and the whole world, to gather them to the battle of that great day of God Almighty.

Behold I come as a thief. Blessed is he that watcheth, and keepeth his garments, lest he walk naked, and they see his shame.
And he gathered them together into a place called in the Hebrew tongue Armageddon.

The three forces or ideologies in Europe, (the prophetic earth of Revelation) caused WWI and WWII. They were: Nazism/Fascism, Muslim Turkey (Turkish Empire then in decline, but more recently a part of what might be called Muslim International), and the Papacy. Britain was allied with Russia in WWII, as combating Nazism/Fascism seemed more urgent that the fear of Communism. All sought power by both force and controlling the mind by their propaganda.

As they brought Europe nearer to war Fascism and Nazism allied themselves as the Axis. The papacy supported this for its own reasons. First it offered the chance of thwarting the spread of Russian communism and atheism that they feared would be out of control. Second it had a good prospect of their being on the winning side when communism, together with Britain, and the Allies were defeated, and

§ Stears. J.M *As Birds Flying* Covenant Publishing Co. Ltd. 121 Low Etherley, Bishop Auckland, Co. Durham. DL14 0HA their reward would be twofold, the protestant churches would be dealt a severe blow, and the British monarchy that had outwitted the Papal power in the Reformation, would be removed.

We are told that these ideologies are motivated by devils. This may sound surprising to some. But consider that this confederacy was intent on destroying both Israel/Britain and the British Empire, and also the Jewish people, particularly in the German dominated countries, in the 'Holocaust', and usurp their roles in God's programme. That would have prevented the formation of the Israeli State, and frustrated the purposes of God. This was anti-semitic, big time. They knew our identity even if our own people do not.

Notice too the purpose God had in allowing this to involve the whole world, from America in the West to Japan in the Far East: it was to bring them to battle against God Himself; bringing them to that point but not yet engaging in that battle, but preparation for it. The only possible historical event, to which this can refer, concluded as WWII.

It is important to cast our minds back to WWI, when the British with Commonwealth help, was fighting in Flanders against Germany, and at the same time in Palestine against the Turks. Then as now Turkey is a Muslim country. WWI hostilities concluded with an armistice, not a peace. It could equally well be said that WWII was the continuation of WWI. This keeps the Muslim forces in the equation, and from the biblical point of view the followers of the false prophet, of which more later.

This reminds us too that God took victory away from the European confederacy unexpectedly, they were sure that they would win, Britain being unprepared.

There is a blessing for those who watch these things, because they will not be deceived or embarrassed by these developments.

It says 'he' gathered them in verse 16, but it says 'they', that is, the three unclean spirits, gathered them in verse 14. We should conclude that the three spirits acted without realising it was the Divine Plan. God ambushing his enemies. But what, or where, is, or was, this rendezvous called Armageddon?

The location is like so much of Revelation symbolic, we know that WWII was not fought in the Vale of Megiddo in Palestine, but part of

WWI. There are many who still expect another great conflict in that place there heralding the return of Christ in glory; this may yet prove to be the case. Let us not jump too far ahead; there is yet one more vial of God's wrath to be poured out. It all depends on what Armageddon means.

The first problem with Megiddo is that it is a very small location in which to visualise modern type long-range battlefield weaponry where the armies of numerous nations are engaged.

The second problem with Megiddo is that the three unclean spirits were the agency by which WWII was brought about, as we saw earlier. After WWII the nations of Europe are again brought together under the Treaty of Rome. Rome the modern symbolic Babylon.

The same spirits have persuaded these former combatants that they are friends, and need each other including Britain, quite a miracle by any standard. The location of this gathering together is once again the prophetic earth of Europe, but their ideologies have also spread world wide, with a view to engulfing the whole world in their schemes. Several other nations have joined the E.U. recently and others including Turkey are hoping to join in an ongoing process. Let us not forget that Turkey was an ally of Germany in W I, and involved earlier in our studies, and the timing of their E.U. entry may be a crucial thing to watch for, as it may also have implications involving other Muslim countries.

This is the prophesied process, and the location is centred on Europe, rather than Palestine.

There is one more clue to Armageddon, we are informed that it is relevant to the Hebrew tongue. This can be regarded as a composite word, in this way:-

a) 'Arma', which is a word for bare grain, as in reaping and threshing. We earlier saw the Russian sickle involved in the gathering of the vine of the earth, a harvesting process.

b) 'Gai', meaning a valley, as in 'valley of decision' see *Joel* 3 v. 16. And the third vial was poured out on the rivers of Europe, all rivers have valleys.

c) 'Don', meaning judgement. God's wrath is judgement, as seen in verse 5 of this chapter. '*Thou art righteous, O Lord ---- because thou hast judged thus'.*

We now have a coded description of the place Armageddon which identifies it by the context, as at least including the European theatre of operations.

It is important to see that these countries that are involved in these events are not doing so, or taking sides because of their own particular programme even if they think so, but are acting out in an involuntary manner the parts that have been ordained of God, very much as an actor in a play represents a character guided by the director, but all follow the plot of the playwright. Remember God's word to Zerubbabel, '*Not by might, nor by power, but by my spirit, saith the Lord of hosts*'. (*Zechariah* 4 v. 6). As we saw, it was the three unclean spirits that deceived the nations, and motivated them for war, and then later deceived them again for peace. How long should we expect this peace engineered by deception to last; and when will there be a falling out?

We may not have much choice about which country we live in, and what its agenda may be, but we do have this important choice; we can make sure that we are right with God, and put our faith in the saving grace of our Lord Jesus Christ.

O°°°°°°°O

From this point on we are at about the transit point between looking at prophecy in hindsight, and looking at things to come. Nearly two millennia ago when John recorded this for us, it was of things shortly to come to pass. Much is now past. There is still some that is shortly to come to pass.

Let us Pray.

Lord Jesus, Who showed these things to your servant John, bless us, and grant us also that measure of your Holy Spirit, and the eye of faith, that we may have a right understanding of Your word, and give glory to Your name, as we see Your purposes come to pass, and Your kingdom coming. Amen.

16 v. 17-19. And the seventh angel poured out his vial into the air; and there came a great voice out of the temple of heaven, and from the throne, saying, It is done.

And there were voices, and thunders, and lightnings; and there was a great earthquake, such as was not since men were upon the earth, so mighty an earthquake, and so great.

And the city was divided into three parts, and the cities of the nations fell: and great Babylon came in remembrance before God, to give unto her the cup of the wine of the fierceness of his wrath.

The seventh vial poured into the air, is as the seventh trumpet followed by thunder, lightning and earthquake. We are being introduced to the final scenes of judgement, hence the emphatic statement; IT IS DONE. All the Babylonian sequence of empires and religious systems and ideologies until Rome, have been brought to the final showdown. As the sacred cups from the Temple of Jerusalem were desecrated at Belshazzar's Feast to toast the idols of Babylon, just before its downfall, so God is returning the compliment with the cup of His wrath, at the imminent collapse of all false and deceptive systems in the world.

This vial and the air indicates the use of air power, or the contamination of the atmosphere, or weapons passing through the air, all of which are possible today; or even some as yet unknown act of God, that we are not able to name.

And what of the earthquake? It is in keeping with the symbolism that it most probably represents great social upheavals, yet it may be predicting a tectonic disaster, perhaps that at Jerusalem and the Mount of Olives at the return of Christ, or a substantial tectonic precursor to that event.

The division of the great city into three parts, also reminds us of the Roman empire being divided and largely destroyed in Chapter 8. We should therefore not be surprised if troubles fall on the modern Roman European systems from three differing sources. It may be that the single currency will become unworkable, causing divisions to occur. Only time will tell.

16 v. 20- 21. And every island fled away, and the mountains were not found.

And there fell upon men a great hail out of heaven, every stone about the weight of a talent: and men blasphemed God because of the plague of the hail; for the plague thereof was exceeding great.

In the symbolism of Revelation , mountains represent nations: when the islands flee away, it may indicate the U.K's rapid withdrawal, or ejection from the E.U. Either in the hope of avoiding conflict or because of a realisation of the deception that caused involvement, or of repentance and wishing to rely on God's power and mercy instead of the E.U. Mountains not found, may mean no longer found united; and possibly because of integration under E.U. Directives, national identities may be hard to define. This could also indicate confusion, with nations frustrated that because of centralisation they may not have the means to carry out any action or policy thought to be in their own interest.

It is also worth noting that in WW II bombs were the bigger the better, but here the weight of a talent, a weight formerly in common use, may indicate such as the cluster bombs used in the Kosovo campaign, or weapons as yet being developed. Sadly Rome will not repent but will blame God for her troubles.

This is a brief introduction to the fall of latter-day Babylon, it is so important that chapters 17 and 18 are devoted to it. Jesus wants us to understand what He is doing, so we will have a series of explanations and details.

Chapter 17

17 v. 1-3. And there came one of the seven angels which had the seven vials, and talked with me, saying unto me, Come hither; I will show unto thee the judgement of the great whore that sitteth upon many waters:

With whom the kings of the earth have committed fornication, and the inhabitants of the earth have been made drunk with the wine of her fornication.

So he carried me away in the spirit into the wilderness: and I saw a woman sit upon a scarlet coloured beast, full of the names of blasphemy, having seven heads and ten horns.

The pouring of the seventh vial was followed by a brief outline of the judgement of Babylon, some times called the 'dooms of Babylon', - all things Roman, political, financial and religious ideology. We are now with John seeing in greater detail, as we are transported to the European wilderness of the prophetical earth, where the great whore has authority. We are looking mainly at the period after WW II, the present and near future.

The symbols in this scene are interesting, the many waters represent a group of nations using various languages, where she has authority, - the European Union under the Treaty of Rome. The kings, that is leaders and representatives of the nations have become infatuated by these newfound powers and are corrupted by them. The entire Council of Ministers resigned in 1999, when a number of them were found to be incompetent or corrupt, - and then they all took their offices back again!

This is the wine of her fornication, the joining nations together in an unnatural manner, and suppressing their traditional differences; it is a deception of man's making and on man's terms. Only God can make all nations join together, and that will only happen under the direction of the Prince of Peace. We saw the red dragon or beast in chapter 12, and it is like the vision of *Daniel* chapter 7. Here the woman is seated on it, that is in charge or control of it.

17 v. 4-6. And the woman was arrayed in purple and scarlet colour, and decked with gold and precious stones and pearls, having a golden cup in her hand full of abominations and filthiness of her fornication:

And upon her forehead was a name written, MYSTERY, BABYLON THE GREAT, THE MOTHER OF HARLOTS AND ABOMINATIONS OF THE EARTH.

And I saw the woman drunken with the blood of the saints, and with the blood of the martyrs of Jesus: and when I saw her I wondered with great admiration.

The purple as of royal authority, scarlet as is worn by cardinals, and costly adornments and garments as of Roman Catholic clergy; what a contrast with the pure white robes of the Saints.

The mystery signifies the nearness to the truth of Rome's teaching, yet containing deliberate errors and idolatry contrived to extract money from and to control their faithful, thus making the whole abominable to God. By contrast, even where errors exist in the Protestant denominations, and some must exist, as they all claim to believe something different, these are not for the purpose of deceit but are derived from outdated understanding of scripture, and cloud the vision of Christ and His purposes.

Here is the important identification mark.

This symbolic woman is responsible for the death of the saints and martyrs of Jesus. Only Rome has killed Christians as a matter of policy, pagan Rome did so out of ignorance of God, and for entertainment. Papal Rome did the same on a larger scale, pretending that they were doing God a service, knowing the truth and ruthlessly suppressing it.

To see the person responsible for some 50,000,000 deaths - not surprising that John, who saw things as if they were actually taking place, was amazed.

17 v. 7-9. And the angel said unto me, Wherefore didst thou marvel? I will tell thee the mystery of the woman, and of the beast that carrieth her, which hath seven heads and ten horns.

The beast that thou sawest was, and is not; and shall ascend out of the bottomless pit, and go into perdition: and they that dwell on the earth shall wonder, whose names were not written in the book of life from the foundation of the world, when they behold the beast that was, and is not, and yet is.

And here is the mind which hath wisdom. The seven heads are seven mountains, on which the woman sitteth.

This is a long-range view from pagan Rome to the present. First, Rome was pagan. Second, pagan Rome no longer exists. Third, it continues to exist as papal Rome. We saw the bottomless pit earlier in chapter 9, from which the Mohammedan or Islamic Faith emerged, now we are being shown that the Roman Catholicism is from similar inspiration. Both were formed near the same time, and the smoke from that pit represents the dark middle ages. Perdition – is a permanent form of death.

The seven heads have two meanings; first, the seven hills on which Rome is built, second, the papacy is the seventh form of Roman Government. Please notice; the true Church of Jesus is not included here, as their names ARE in the Lamb's Book of Life.

At the time of the Reformation these things were understood. The Pope identified as the man of sin, in the Dedicatory Letter in the King James Bible, and many errors were removed in the newly reformed church. Since then there has been a gradual regression towards accepting the old Roman ways.

17 v. 10-11. And there are seven kings: five are fallen, and one is, and the other is not yet come; and when he cometh, he must continue a short space.

And the beast that was, and is not, even he is the eighth, and is of the seven, and goeth into perdition.

It may look complicated, but it is clear and easy to see. At the time of John, five kings or forms of Roman government were past. Caesar was the head of state in his time, so the Caesars were the sixth form or type. The Papacy followed being therefore the seventh type. The beast is the eighth, and is the instruments set up by its predecessor, from the Lateran Councils to the Treaty of Rome and its Council of Ministers. These are supposedly independent to deceive those who would not like the Roman Church to control their political, religious and economic destiny.

God has plainly warned us of these things.

17 v. 12-13. And the ten horns which thou sawest are ten kings, which have received no kingdom as yet; but receive power as kings one hour with the beast.

These have one mind, and shall give their power and strength unto the beast.

The ten horns follow the same pattern as before, but now the vision is worldwide. This is a reconstituted beast image, and the horns represent a new set of nations or groups of nations. This is a future development, whereby these ten will be developed and hope to have great power as kings, and all wholeheartedly agree to support the Babylon type economic/religious system. Their leaders look forward to great rewards, and will receive their powers, but the privilege will be short lived to one prophetic hour. By Revelation's time scale of a day representing an actual year, this is only going to be a few weeks. These things may represent the division of the world into ten Economic Regions or Kingdoms, as proposed by the Club of Rome. Is the E.U. being the pattern piece for the other nine?

17 v. 14-18. These shall make war with the Lamb, and the Lamb shall overcome them: for he is Lord of lords, and King of kings: and they that are with him are called, and chosen, and faithful.

And he saith unto me, The waters which thou sawest, where the whore sitteth, are peoples, and multitudes, and nations, and tongues.

And the ten horns which thou sawest upon the beast, these shall hate the whore, and shall make her desolate and naked, and shall eat her flesh, and burn her with fire.

For God hath put in their hearts to fulfil his will, and to agree, and give their kingdom unto the beast, until the words of God shall be fulfilled.

And the woman which thou sawest is that great city, which reigneth over the kings of the earth.

This new ten horns controlled by the beast, is in turn ridden or controlled by the woman, and proceeds to war against the Lamb. Since it is not possible to attack Jesus while He remains in heaven, and we are not yet told that the Second Advent has occurred, this must mean an orchestrated attack on His two witnesses, church and state. We saw earlier that Israel/Britain may have made a withdrawal from the E.U. Similarly other Israel nations worldwide may also withdraw from their respective horn Kingdoms and re-form their own Commonwealth Union. This may be the cause of conflict, and/or trade sanctions. The King of kings will ensure that in whatever form this action may be against His chosen, it will be disastrous.

Coming face to face with Christ's power will enlighten and reveal to the ten horns of the beast, the deceptions of the Babylon/Roman system, and their loyalty will turn to hatred, there does not seem to be any indication that their loyalty will be to Christ because they perform the destiny He prepared for them. The fact that they will have suffered severe losses because of deception will motivate them for revenge, and possibly without realising it will perform God's Will in destroying Babylon, the great whore, just as she appeared to have gained control of the whole world.

Jesus had something to say about the dangers of gaining the whole world. (*Mark* 8 v. 36).

Chapter 18

18 v.1-33. And after these things I saw another angel come down from heaven, having great power; and the earth was lightened with his glory.

And he cried mightily with a strong voice, saying, Babylon the great is fallen, is fallen, and is become the habitation of devils, and the hold of every foul spirit, and a cage of every unclean and hateful bird.

For all nations have drunk of the wine of the wrath of her fornication, and the kings of the earth have committed fornication with her, and the merchants of the earth are waxed rich through the abundance of her delicacies.

There is only One who enlightens the earth with His glory, our Lord Himself. But it says, after these things. Which things? It could mean those we have just looked at in chapter 17, or that which is about to be described throughout this chapter 18. We may be certain it is not telling us that the Second Advent will be predictable by observing the events of this prophecy, beyond indicating that it is associated with the period of the dooms of Babylon.

As we have seen, Rome will have spread its net to include all nations and the process of removing and reversing that will take some time. We are being shown stages and aspects of this, and the demise of the vested interests.

18 v. 4. And I heard another voice from heaven, saying, Come out of her, my people, that ye be not partakers of her sins, and that ye receive not of her plagues.

Come out of her My people... Another voice, certainly a contrasting tone of voice, not now proclaiming doom, but the loving and caring voice of the Saviour, calling His people to Himself, that they might avoid coming troubles. Who are, My people? Are they not the same as those with whom God made covenants and redeemed them so that they may be His people, and serve only His purposes. As the plagues of Egypt led to the redemption of Israel so also will the plagues of modern Babylon.

18 v. 5- 8.   For her sins have reached unto heaven, and God hath remembered her iniquities. Reward her even as she rewarded you, and double unto her double according to her works: in the cup which she hath filled full to her double.

How much she hath glorified herself, and lived deliciously, so much torment and sorrow give her: for she saith in her heart, I sit a queen, and am no widow, and shall see no sorrow.

Therefore shall her plagues come in one day, death, and mourning, and famine; and she shall be utterly burned with fire: for strong is the Lord God who judgeth her.

The number of doubles implies absolute certainty, and the one hour that tells us that these events will take only a short period to bring about the total collapse of all that is called Babylon.

18 v. 9-19.   And the kings of the earth, who have committed fornication and lived deliciously with her, shall bewail her, and lament for her, when they see the smoke of her burning,

Standing afar off for the fear of her torment, saying, Alas, alas, that great city Babylon, that mighty city! For in one hour is thy judgement come.

And the merchants of the earth shall weep and mourn over her; for no man buyeth their merchandise any more:

The merchandise of gold, and silver, and precious stones, and of pearls, and fine linen, and purple, and silk, and scarlet, and all thyine wood, and all manner vessels of ivory, and all manner vessels of most precious wood, and of brass, and iron, and marble,

And cinnamon, and odours, and ointments, and frankincense, and wine, and oil, and fine flour, and wheat, and beasts, and sheep, and horses, and chariots, and slaves, and souls of men.

And the fruits that thy soul lusteth after are departed from thee, and all things which were dainty and goodly are departed from thee, and thou shalt find them no more at all.

The merchants of these things, which were made rich by her, shall stand afar off for fear of her torment, weeping and wailing,

And saying, Alas, alas, that great city, that was clothed in fine linen, and purple, and scarlet, and decked with gold, and precious stones, and pearls!

For in one hour so great riches is come to nought. And every shipmaster, and all the company in ships, and sailors, and as many as trade by sea, stood afar off,

And cried when they saw the smoke of her burning, saying, What city is like unto this great city!

And they cast dust on their heads, and cried, weeping and wailing, and saying, Alas, alas, that great city, wherein were made rich all that had ships in the sea by reason of her costliness! For in one hour is she made desolate.

This clearly indicates the collapse of world trade and big business, and finance based on debt and usury that God forbids. The Papal religious system makes money from the souls of the dear departed. The smoke may be the reward for the burning of martyrs, but probably indicates the impact of bombs or missiles. Alternatively this could be earthquake damage as indicated in chapter 16 v. 18, but it would not by itself conform to the ten kings' rebellion. We must wait and see how it works out.

18 v. 20. Rejoice over her, thou heaven, and ye holy apostles and prophets; for God hath avenged you on her.

This is a further response to chapter 6 v. 9-11, all the martyrs and those who have lost their lives opposing evil and oppressive regimes.

18 v. 21-24. And a mighty angel took up a stone like a great millstone, and cast it into the sea, saying, Thus with violence shall that great city Babylon be thrown down, and shall be found no more at all.

And the voice of harpers, and musicians, and of pipers, and trumpeters, shall be heard no more at all in thee; and no craftsman, of whatsoever craft he be, shall be found any more in thee; and the sound of a millstone shall be heard no more at all in thee;

And the light of a candle shall shine no more at all in thee; and the voice of the bridegroom and of the bride shall be heard no more at all in thee: for thy merchants were the great men of the earth; for by thy sorceries were all nations deceived.

And in her was found the blood of prophets, and saints, and all that were slain upon the earth.

All this destruction, however caused will be complete, and irreversible. Our concern should be for the many survivors of this catastrophe. It would seem that the Second Advent occurs at about the time of these events, as the following Chapter 19 includes much rejoicing and preparations for the marriage of the Lamb, as well as the mopping up that concludes the fall of Babylon. Let us pray that Christ will direct us towards that great responsibility of reconstruction under his guidance to His glory.

Chapter 19

19 v. 1- 3.And after these things I heard a great voice of much people in heaven, saying, Alleluia; Salvation, and glory, and honour, and power, unto the Lord our God:

For true and righteous are his judgements: for he hath judged the great whore, which did corrupt the earth with her fornication, and hath avenged the blood of his servants at her hand.

And again they said, Alleluia. And her smoke rose up for ever and ever.

Well might we expect there to be a round of praise and worship in the heavens, as the enemy of God's people is judged. There will be on earth also when this becomes accomplished, especially in Israel/Britain and her family of Christian nations, when the reality of Divine intervention and release from Babylonian oppression is discovered; there will be great praise and rejoicing before God for His redemption, and saving grace. The ascending smoke to remind that all man's efforts if without God's blessing are as dust and ashes.

19 v.4- 6. And the four and twenty elders and the four beasts fell down and worshipped God that sat on the throne, saying, Amen; Alleluia.

And a voice came out of the throne, saying, Praise our God, all ye his servants, and ye that fear him, both small and great.

And I heard as it were the voice of a great multitude, and as the voice of many waters, and as the voice of mighty thunderings, saying, Alleluia: for the Lord God the omnipotent reigneth.

A further round of praise, and a call to all who fear God. This may be an invitation to the millions who call themselves Christian, and fear God, but because all deceptions are removed, will have lost their church, or it is discredited, and will not be sure where to worship, or how. Where else could an invitation come from but the throne, the throne of David is in a unique position to do this; it may be from Christ Himself, who may by then be installed on His hereditary throne. Something must be done, they cannot be left as sheep without a shepherd. Then will be that great paean of praise to echo that in the heavens as Christian unity under Christ becomes a reality.

19 v. 7. Let us be glad and rejoice, and give honour to him: for the marriage of the Lamb is come, and his wife hath made herself ready.

The marriage of the Lamb is a great and important forthcoming event.

As with ordinary marriages, it is the result of courtship and developing love, which takes some time to reach fruition. In this case it has taken a long time, and the Bride has been many times unresponsive to, and rejective of, the Bridegroom's overtures, while He has had to take the most extreme measures to overcome difficulties and problems to convey His everlasting love, in order to fulfil their combined destiny. It is the summit of a love story that runs throughout the Bible, and is often misunderstood by Christians of all varieties. We need first to identify the Bridegroom and the Bride.

The Lamb is easy, it is none other than the Lord Jesus, a title that is used to denote Him particularly when His sacrificial and redemptive role is indicated. He is the Lamb slain from the foundation of the world, as we saw in chapter 13 v. 8, and His resurrection power is implied, and His sufferings were expected and described as in *Isaiah* 53.

The concept of God being married was taught by the Old Testament prophets. The relationship between God and the house of Israel is mentioned in *Jeremiah* 31 v. 32, *'...although I was an husband unto them, saith the Lord'*, *Isaiah* 50 refers to the divorced state; also *'...For thy Maker is thine husband.'* (*Isaiah* 54 v. 5).

Hosea's prophecy is an allegory of the adulterous Northern House of Israel divorced by God, disgraced and seemingly lost, yet He is determined to have her, and later to get her back.

In spite of such plain statements many Christians are unsure what this marriage is. Some suppose it is the 'Rapture' when Christ returns and takes us all up to heaven. What a wonderful idea, but this person has not found any substantial biblical support for this. Meeting Him in the clouds, yes, but the clouds are a vital part of the earthly environment, and not heaven.

Jesus said, *'...in the resurrection they neither marry, nor are given in marriage'*, (*Matthew* 22 v. 30). So this is not the same as a marriage of a man with a woman, for Jesus is already resurrected. That is the vital point, the marriage of the Lamb concerns One who is resurrected, that is God in the person of the Lord Jesus. But consider this! Isaiah also said after describing a time of troubles:

Isaiah 26 v. 19. Thy dead men shall live, together with my dead body shall they arise. Awake and sing; ye that dwell in the dust: for thy dew is as the dew of herbs, and the earth shall cast out the dead.

Alternative readings –

Schofield- :-
Thy dead shall live: my dead bodies shall rise...

Ferrar Fenton- :-
Your dead shall live, your corpses rise;
Awake and cheer who sleep in dust,
The morning's dew shall drop on you,
But earth o'erwhelm the oppressors.

Thus when Christ returns, it is not just the faithful living, but also of the faithful dead He claims that 'my dead bodies shall rise'! If you rise at His signal, or if you are changed at His appearing, then you will be among those ready for, and party to that great event that follows.

We are also informed that, *'...his wife hath made herself ready'.* Thus we see that the bride is also the wife, that is the same that was, before the divorce. Making herself ready to be joined to the Lord of glory implies that her former adulterous state is repented of, forgiven, and in the past, and Israel is ready for full unwavering commitment to the Lord.

19 v. 8. And to her was granted that she should be arrayed in fine linen, clean and white: for the fine linen is the righteousness of saints.

That is self-explanatory, it is just saying that she is covered by the Lord's righteousness. Not her own.

19 v. 9. And he saith unto me, Write, Blessed are they, which are called unto the marriage supper of the Lamb. And he saith unto me, These are true sayings of God.

Notice that there is no indication here that this is to take place in heaven. We may presume that preparations for this will take place, you know the sort of things that we do for an ordinary marriage. The Bride we saw was covered with the garment of righteousness, that is, saved by the precious blood of Jesus, and covered by the New Covenant, a fact that they and we celebrate in Holy Communion from time to time. We should all consider the New Covenant and determine with whom it is made. Old and New Testaments agree:-

> *Jeremiah 31 v. 31. Behold, the days come, saith the LORD, that I will make a new covenant with the house of Israel, and with the house of Judah:*

> *Hebrews 8 v. 10. For this is the covenant that I will make with the house of Israel after those days, saith the Lord; I will put my laws into their mind, and write them in their hearts: And I will be to them a God, and they shall be to me a people:*

These scriptures make it quite clear that the New Covenant is with the House of Israel, Jeremiah considers Israel and Judah as distinct entities, as they were in his day, yet in *Hebrews* Israel only is mentioned; what happened to Judah? Are we to see this as indicating that Israel and Judah will be united by the time of the Marriage of the Lamb? Ezekiel said it would happen in the vision of two sticks, (chapter 37). If that is so, then the House of Judah will have accepted Jesus of Nazareth as their messiah and mediator of that New Covenant by the time of the fulfilment of this prophecy. So we know we have some time to wait for that, but we know that we are looking at a promise of the future, and we are looking at the future as indicated by God's certain Word.

We should see this as the grafting in of the cut off branches off the Israel olive tree, as described in *Romans* 11, and the new life given to the dead branches. Nowhere are we to find the New Covenant was made with the Church, but the Church as the body of believers is embraced by it, and therefore a vitally integral part of the Israel Kingdom.

> *19 v. 10. And I fell at his feet to worship him. And he said unto me, See thou do it not: I am thy fellow servant, and of thy brethren that have the testimony of Jesus: worship God: for the testimony of Jesus is the spirit of prophecy.*

John is so overjoyed at this news, that all Israel is to be reunited by Christ that he attempted to worship the angel who gave him this news. Isn't it wonderful to know that these well informed angels are our fellow servants, they work with and for us.

19 v. 11-16. And I saw heaven opened, and behold a white horse; and he that sat upon him was called Faithful and True, and in righteousness he doth judge and make war.

His eyes were as a flame of fire, and on his head were many crowns; and he had a name written, that no man knew, but he himself.

And he was clothed with a vesture dipped in blood: and his name is called The Word of God.

And the armies which were in heaven followed him upon white horses, clothed in fine linen, white and clean.

And out of his mouth goeth a sharp sword, that with it he should smite the nations: and he shall rule them with a rod of iron: and he treadeth the winepress of the fierceness and wrath of Almighty God.

And he hath on his vesture and on his thigh a name written, KING OF KINGS, AND LORD OF LORDS.

This vision may be another viewpoint or overlapping view of what we saw as the destruction of 'Babylon', but this time showing the returned Christ's active role. Contrasting chapter 17 v. 16-17, where we were told, 'God hath put it in their (the horns) hearts to fulfil his will'. If this is the case, the confederacy of the ten horns, will only partly destroy the great whore before the returned Christ takes charge. A limit being imposed by Him for the degree of permitted human vengeance. We are not told at what point Christ will return, and bring heavenly hosts, beyond the appearance of being related to that event the duration of which we do not know. His garment is marked with the blood of His enemies, as He subdues them and brings the chaos to order. The winepress of the fierceness of the wrath of Almighty God, is a very ominous symbol, and looks very like World War III. In His mercy may it not last long. The iron rod is thought by some to be un-Christ like, not thought to be compatible with the gentle Jesus concept. We must consider that iron represents unbending strength, and therefore it describes Christ's administration as strong and just and impartial.

There emerges an interesting situation, in chapter 17 v. 14, we have the ten horns acting under the influence of the great whore making war against the Lamb, if not against Him personally then against His Elect, and then in verse 16, these same ten horns are shown as hating the whore and destroying her. They seem to be on both sides! This may be intended to show us the degree of high-powered deceptions among nations, and what will happen when those deceptions are exposed. Verse 17 makes it clear that this strange situation is God's will, and they are fulfilling His purpose. Here in chapter 19 we see the closing stages of this drama.

19 v.17-19. And I saw an angel standing in the sun; and he cried with a loud voice, saying to all the fowls that fly in the midst of heaven, Come and gather yourselves together unto the supper of the great God;

That ye may eat the flesh of kings, and the flesh of captains, and the flesh of mighty men, and the flesh of horses, and of them that sit on them, and the flesh of all men, both free and bond, both small and great.

And I saw the beast, and the kings of the earth, and their armies, gathered together to make war against him that sat on the horse, and against his army.

Some suppose this to be the battle of Armageddon, but the description here would fit the many times prophesied battle of the great day of God. There has never been anything remotely like it, and thank God that Jesus will be in sole control.

19 v. 20-21. And the beast was taken, and with him the false prophet that wrought miracles before him, with which he deceived them that had received the mark of the beast, and them that worshipped his image.

These both were cast alive into a lake of fire burning with brimstone.

And the remnant were slain with the sword of him that sat upon the horse, which sword proceeded out of his mouth: and all the fowls were filled with their flesh.

This is an important message for our information and guidance today.

The beast is the Roman system, especially papal and E.U.; also elsewhere called Babylon, 13 v. 1-3.

The false prophet - the motivation of the Muslim system, also occupying much of the territory that was once the Babylonian Empire - 9 v. 1- 6.

Both originated or came to prominence around the same time, and are together disposed of by Christ in person!

Time will tell if this hypothesis is correct, as with all prophecy only the fulfilment can decide for certain, but is given to guide and warn us of things that will shortly come to pass. Are we here being shown that at the time when the false aspects of these systems are being discovered with a general uprising probably firstly against Roman or E.U. centralisation, that there will be some sort of unholy alliance between the Papacy or Romanism and the Muslim powers, as they are shown as being disposed of together. For this to be correct we need to identify the miracles performed by the false prophet, in support of the beast. What does this mean? Does Turkey's desired entry into E.U. hold the key? Is it one of the miracles, the unprecedented influx of Muslim/Islamic immigrants into the core of the Protestant West, as being supposedly peaceful? Anyone observing the recent Muslim conduct in Iraq and placards on the London streets early in 2006, will see the 'peaceful' potential for Britain!

Unlikely as this alliance may seem to some at present, there are important common factors that would make their union easy; the use of force throughout their history in various forms to promote their causes, and both are expansionists and both the cause of spiritual darkness, and both seek to destroy the true Christian faith. When deceptions are exposed, they may well take the view that joining forces would be their best option. Has this already secretly happened? By uniting the power of the E.U. with the oil wealth of the Middle East, who would be able to oppose them? Will Russia outwit them? It would indeed be a formidable force either way ranged against what will be left of the Protestant West.

However this may be, happily, we are told that the returned Christ is able to deal with that and any situation.

We have been looking at some of the events that will occur at or soon after the return of Christ. The construction of *Revelation* describes events individually but often they are overlapping at least in part.

We are not given an exact timetable, but it is written for our guidance and to support our faith, especially in days of spiritual darkness. May its Author graciously enlighten us according to our needs.

Although *Revelation* seems to omit the advance by Russia, or Gog and confederates, as indicated in *Ezekiel* 38 & 39, it is hard to imagine that the opportunity presented by the European falling out and conflict against Babylon would not be missed. What a golden opportunity when all eyes are focussed elsewhere to make their move. We have seen previously that Revelation concentrates more on the European sector, and its internal strife. We should also keep our minds open to Ezekiel's prophecy being fulfilled during or near these things. In the first few days of 2006, a cold shiver went right through Europe as Russia, who sells gas to many countries, turned off some supplies to the Ukraine to apply economic and political pressure. Moscow has now tested a very powerful weapon; fortunately Britain draws very marginally on that source.

Chapter 20

20 v. 1- 3.   And I saw an angel come down from heaven, having the key to the bottomless pit and a great chain in his hand.

And he laid hold on the dragon, that old serpent, which is the Devil, and Satan, and bound him a thousand years,

And cast him into the bottomless pit, and shut him up, and set a seal upon him, that he should deceive the nations no more, till the thousand years should be fulfilled: and after that he must be loosed a little season.

If one was to make a list of those things that relate to Our Lord's return, and try to put them into some sort of order of importance, most would put the removal of Satan from our lives at least in the upper half. It is hard to imagine the transformation that would result if that was the only event of importance. Just think for a moment how the world around us would be changed without the source of the inspiration behind the destructive forces of hatred and greed. Yet couple that with the transformation resulting from the righteous rule of Christ, and we are going beyond anything that our experience can adequately put words to. With such major changes it would be useless to speculate.

There is however one ominous note! After a thousand years Satan is to be briefly released. We will see why later.

20 v. 4.   And I saw thrones, and they sat upon them, and judgement was given unto them: and I saw the souls of them that were beheaded for the witness of Jesus, and for the word of God, and which had not worshipped the beast, neither his image, neither had received his mark upon their foreheads, or in their hands; and they lived and reigned with Christ a thousand years.

There are thrones, with people sitting on them. We are not told how many thrones there are, but two numbers present themselves as possible. We saw in the vision 24 seated elders round God's throne in chapter 4, which may be the pattern followed here: or probably 12 as described by Jesus in *Matthew* 19 v. 28 where He states that the apostles will sit on 12 thrones judging the tribes of Israel.

Is this the marriage of the Lamb? In marriage as we know it husband and wife share all, whether good fortune or bad, and their first thoughts are for each other, and they like nothing more than being together. We call it love and hope it will last a lifetime.

We are shown an assembly of those who showed their love of Jesus, for life. They showed their love even to death, and against all kinds of terrible adversities, of which the apostles were among the first in following the example of their Lord. He therefore declares that they are worthy to be our judges, which may also imply administrators. We know that there were vast numbers who lost their lives because they opposed the beast, over many centuries, and many others who lived lives of faithfulness devoted to Jesus by preserving, publishing and translating of the gospel, who are raised in this first resurrection. Also the living faithful will be changed to join that throng.

For so many to be expressing their love and be ever united with the Lord, is a relationship that defies the use of any other word or concept known to us except marriage.

20 v. 5-6. But the rest of the dead lived not again until the thousand years were finished. This is the first resurrection.

Blessed and holy is he that hath part in the first resurrection: on such the second death hath no power, but they shall be priests of God and of Christ, and shall reign with him a thousand years.

Christ will occupy the throne of David as prophesied, (*Luke* 1 v. 32 – 33). This has been preserved through long ages, and is at present the throne of Great Britain, and now in the custody of Her Majesty Queen Elizabeth II, of the line of David**.

From the foregoing we find that at the return of Christ, to which all denominations of Christians look every time they celebrate Holy Communion, and declare their belief in the raising of the dead, is intrinsic with the marriage of the Lamb, and the setting up by Him of an organised form of government, as prophesied that He would do. *'The government shall be upon his shoulder'* (*Isaiah* 9 v. 6). Therefore those who are part of the first resurrection are blessed by being priests of God

---

** Royal House of Britain an Enduring Dynasty + Chart, W.M.H. Milner, C.P.C. 121 Low Etherley, Bishop Auckland, Co. Durham, DL14 0HA.

and Christ. They therefore perform priestly duties, and this will include taking the gospel to those who are not Christ's at His coming, but survive the turmoil of the falling out among nations, and carnage that will occur near the time of Christ's return. They will find themselves becoming subject to His righteous administration for the next thousand years, certainly not part of it without conversion. Mankind's period of doing as they please will have ended.

The most vital aspect of the millennium is that the Laws of God will be administered and fully observed, to the righting of all wrongs, allowing enormous blessings and prosperity.

The remaining dead do not take part in these things, but must wait until after the millennial reign of Christ. Then we will see what the second death is.

20 v. 7-10.   And when the thousand years are expired. Satan shall be loosed out of his prison,

And shall go out to deceive the nations which are in the four quarters of the earth, Gog and Magog, to gather them together to battle: the number of whom is as the sand of the sea.

And they went up on the breadth of the earth, and compassed the camp of the saints about, and the beloved city: and fire came down from God out of heaven, and devoured them.

And the devil that deceived them was cast into the lake of fire and brimstone, where the beast and the false prophet are, and shall be tormented day and night forever and ever.

A thousand years on, and the key to Satan's prison had not been lost. One wonders why not! The mention of Gog and Magog may mean that Russia is mostly referred to here, for Satan resumes his work of deception, evidently unrepentant after imprisonment. Yet this is more far reaching than just Russia, for Satan's deception reaches round the globe, it would appear that there is still at least a residual element of atheism or communism of a very widespread nature. A thousand years of peace and plenty will produce a large population explosion. Without leadership, this ungodly element has presumably been quiescent throughout the millennial reign of peace, but spontaneously rises to Satan's lead, and is promptly and divinely dealt with.

It is evident from this that human nature will be unchanged by the benefits of Christ's millennial rule, will still be self-willed and rebellious to the point of self destruction, and will remain in need of the saving grace of the Lord Jesus. Satan is sent to join the false prophet and the beast, for ever and ever, a term that may not be the same as eternal, meaning for ages, or as long as God's purpose for them takes.

20 v. 11-13. And I saw a great white throne, and him that sat on it, from whose face the earth and the heaven fled away; and there was found no place for them.

And I saw the dead, small and great, stand before God; and the books were opened: and another book was opened, which is the book of life: and the dead were judged out of those things that were written in the books, according to their works.

And the sea gave up the dead which were in it; and death and hell delivered up the dead which were in them: and they were judged every man according to their works.

This is the judgement seat of Christ, the dead are raised, this is the second resurrection, and there is an order in which this takes place. See I *Corinthians* 15 v. 22-23. A vital point in the work of Christ seems generally to be missed. It is commonly taught that the Age of Grace ends at the return of Christ, and those not saved by that time are eternally lost. But look at this, the book of Life is again open. It is not for the judgement of Christians as they are already with the Lord, and fear no condemnation. See *Romans* 8 v. 1. It is therefore open to receive the names of certain ones who Christ counts as worthy. We are given some clues as to who the favoured ones may be.

That there will be some surprises in store is evident from the words of Jesus, the Parable of the sheep and goats in *Matthew* 25, shows that those who may not have confessed Christ or even heard of Him, yet lived by the Kingdom principles of showing love to their neighbour, and are rewarded by being given their inheritance in His kingdom. Although this parable refers to the division of nations, and that some observed Christ's kingdom rule of 'love your neighbour' seemingly in ignorance, yet He will welcome them into His kingdom. This may refer to the several Israel nations, and Christ is seen in this parable as distinguishing between them and other nations. The promises to the sons of Jacob make it clear that there will be several nations that constitute all Israel. Paul in *Romans* 11 v. 26- 29 explains this.

So this is not a case of letting sinners into the kingdom, but a case of God keeping His Word to their ancestors whom he loved. This is a self-imposed obligation for God to do this. At what stage this event occurs in the programme of the returned Christ may not be clear to us yet, but it will take place, and as Israel was in Old Testament writings regarded as God's wife, we should expect it to be linked to the marriage of the Lamb. It may fit better in a later context!

The order of events continue with the sea giving up the dead in it. Vast numbers have died in the sea through all history to our own day. The same with death and hell, this must include all who have ever lived. All these to be judged by their works, or how they lived their lives. In this there are factors to consider.

First these people are now alive, presumably knowing their own minds, and being able to answer for themselves.

Second those who have been with Christ during the millennium are priests of God, these would be failing in their priestly duties if they did not explain to all these raised ones who Jesus is, and the work that he has done because of His love for His creation. To teach that it is better to come before Christ in reverence and penitence and seek His mercy, rather than attempt to flee from Him, for there is no hiding place left.

Third the justice and equity of Christ's rule requires that His saving grace will be available to all, regardless of the historical period or location of their past lives.

The raised one would then be in an equal position to all of us now, the choice of seeking Christ's forgiveness and bowing the knee to him, their names then being entered in the book of life, - or not, Christ judging them by their records as he sees fit, for he will have the last word.

20 v. 14-15. And death and hell were cast into the lake of fire. This is the second death.

And whosoever was not found written in the book of life was cast into the lake of fire.

A very ignominious end to all who have determined to oppose God and Christ to the bitter end. The good thing about it is that death has been disposed of. God's judgements are always to produce our long-term benefits. Cast into that lake of fire, which is created and fuelled by the power of God; is it just possible that this is an extreme cleansing process?

We are just not told.

In all processes there is some waste, in order to make the finished product. So in this case; in the beginning within the Garden of Eden, God placed the tree of the knowledge of good and evil.

He created evil (*Job* 31 v. 3). *'Is not destruction to the wicked? And a strange punishment to the workers of iniquity'*? (II *Thessalonians* 1 v. 8 – 9). '...*vengeance on them that know not God, and that obey not the gospel of our Lord Jesus Christ: Who shall be punished with everlasting destruction from the presence of the Lord...*' Many believe that Jesus worked as a carpenter: if so, even in His perfect hands the making of a chair or yoke for oxen required removal of cuttings and shavings, all wasted parts of good wood removed to produce the perfected shapes. Were they not burned to heat mother Mary's cooking pot?

Chapter 21

21 v. 1-2. And I saw a new heaven and a new earth: for the first heaven and the first earth were passed away; and there was no more sea.

And I John saw the holy city, new Jerusalem, coming down from God out of heaven, prepared as a bride adorned for her husband.

We are still with John as he observes and records this great prophetic vision. The passing away of heaven and earth were mentioned in *Revelation 6 v. 14, 'heaven departed as a scroll when it is rolled together; and every mountain and island were moved out of their places'.* This describes a great cataclysmic event, a complete makeover. This raises many more questions than it gives answers. All we see is the beginning of a completely new era, where God is active, and provides a brand new holy Jerusalem, coming down from heaven. Notice this holy city comes from heaven, so heaven must still exist regardless of being new. So also earth remains, reformed, with men, presumably including women. Conditions will be very different with no sea, lots of extra land surface, and a very changed climate. We worry about climate change. Don't worry, it is God's work and we will love it.

It looks as if there is to be another marriage, for the city is prepared as a bride. We come to examine these things in greater detail.

21 v. 3-4. And I heard a great voice out of heaven saying, Behold, the tabernacle of God is with men, and he will dwell with them, and they shall be his people, and God himself shall be with them, and be their God.

And God will wipe away all tears from their eyes; and there shall be no more death, neither sorrow, nor crying, neither shall there be any more pain: for the former things are passed away.

Now we can see why heaven is rolled up like a scroll. It is no longer needed as God's principle home, He is moving. He will dwell with men, this should also make it clear to us that this is on earth, which is to be radically transformed and cleansed of all things which pertain to sin, death and corruption, in preparation for this. His care in wiping away tears, an expression like parental love, shows that He is no longer the awesome judge, but caring father and companion.

21 v. 5-8. And he that sat upon the throne said, Behold, I make all things new. And he said unto me,

Write: for these words are true and faithful.

And he said unto me, It is done. I am Alpha and Omega, the beginning and the end. I will give unto him that is athirst of the fountain of the water of life freely.

He that overcometh shall inherit all things; and I will be his God, and he shall be my son.

But the fearful, and unbelieving, and the abominable, and murderers, and whoremongers, and sorcerers, and idolaters, and all liars, shall have their part in the lake which burneth with fire and brimstone: which is the second death.

These verses take us back to the beginning of the vision, the Lord Jesus, the beginning and the end, as in chapter 1; also in *Hebrews* 12 v. 2. In other words, *'the author and finisher of our faith'*. As the end of this vision draws into focus we are reminded of the situation as it started, and how by God's grace the earth is being made a fit place for God and man to live together in harmony.

21 v. 9-1. And there came unto me one of the seven angels which had the seven vials full of the seven last plagues, and talked with me, saying, Come hither, I will shew thee the bride, the Lamb's wife.

And he carried me away in the spirit to a great and high mountain, and showed me that great city, the holy Jerusalem, descending out of heaven from God,

Having the glory of God: and her light was like a stone most precious, even like a jasper stone, clear as crystal;

Verse 9 has caused concern, sometimes regarded academically as a scribal error, and probably belonging between verse 3 & 4 of Chapter 19. Why this suggestion should be made is not clear, does placing it in the earlier part of Chapter 19 make better sense? The problem is that we are shown a second bride of the Lamb. If there seems to be a problem with this verse, for the moment, suppose for 'Lamb' we substitute 'LORD', in the mind, as meaning Jehovah as often used in O.T. Both are persons of the Godhead. Jesus said, '*I and the Father are one*'. There seem to be these two possibilities:-

First, the following verses are a restatement or new viewpoint as in chapter 19.

Second, this is a separate and distinct event.

If you favour the first just consider the two views as two accounts of the same and add them together in your mind for the overall effect. Secondly think of them as distinct visions. In that case it represents the remarriage of Jehovah to Israel, as Christ was previously seen united with His faithful church. The Old and New Testament concepts brought together as a single God-centred wholeness. Possibly the better view?

We see a great sight, the holy City New Jerusalem, coming out of heaven from God. No man made city this, the work of God no less. Its architect and maker is God. It has the brightness and glory of God, it is pure and crystal clear. God's gift of Himself to mankind; as is Christ.

21 v. 12-14. And had a wall great and high, and had twelve gates, and at the gates twelve angels, and names written thereon, which are the names of the twelve tribes of the children of Israel:

On the east three gates; on the north three gates; on the south three gates; and on the west three gates.

And the wall of the city had twelve foundations, and in them the names of the twelve apostles of the Lamb.

The symbolism of this magnificent City, is shown in motion from God, heaven to earth. God's will and purpose is demonstrated and put into being in the way that it is constructed. Yet it is far more than a symbol it is a reality, and the focal point of things yet more remarkable.

21 v. 15-21. And he that talked with me had a golden reed to measure the city, and the gates thereof, and the wall thereof.

And the city lieth foursquare, and the length is as large as the breadth: and he measured the city with the reed, twelve thousand furlongs. The length and the breadth and the height of it are equal.

And he measured the wall thereof, and hundred and forty and four cubits, according to the measure of a man, that is, of the angel.

And the building of the wall was of jasper: and the city was pure gold, like unto clear glass.

And the foundations of the wall of the city were garnished with all manner of precious stones. The first foundation was jasper; the second, sapphire; the third, chalcedony; the fourth, an emerald;

The fifth, sardonyx; the sixth, sardius; the seventh, chrysolyte; the eighth, beryl; the ninth, a topaz; the tenth, a chrysoprasus; the eleventh, a jacinth; the twelfth, an amethyst.

And the twelve gates were twelve pearls; every several gate was one pearl: and the street of the city was pure gold, as it were transparent glass.

The city's robust construction is beyond human art. It has twelve gates, securely monitored by angels. Each gate is named after one of the tribes of Israel, three on each side, after the manner of the formation of Israel's camp in the wilderness (*Numbers* 2.) The walls are securely built on twelve foundations, each named after an apostle of Jesus; the garnishing stones bear similarity with the stones of the high priest's breastplate (*Exodus* 29). The equality of the height, length and breadth make it a cube or a pyramid. The size is immense, taken literally that is 1500 miles, even if that means the sum of the fours side it is 373 miles for each side, and height. Over 140,000 sq miles of floor space. There are at least two important factors. First the gates are named after the tribes of Israel. Second the foundations are representative of the twelve apostles. At this point we need to notice that those who are in Christ are counted as Abraham's seed. (*Galatians* 3 v. 25) This is the adoption or grafting on to Israel, as heirs of the promises, discussed in *Romans* 9 & 11. No entry except through Israel. No enduring city without the atoning work of Christ as delivered to us through the apostles, as no structure will stand without foundations. Remember the New Covenant is made with Israel, not the Church. (*Jeremiah* 31 & *Hebrews* 8) Thus we see that the covenant and the atoning work of Christ are united in this place of perfection prepared for all the faithful to dwell in with God. In love and mercy and at great cost God has reversed the fall with its shameful consequences.

The pure gold of the streets, not only indicates purity and holiness, but the paving of streets with gold is a term taken to mean a place of

107

great prosperity, the fulfilment of a promise for the keeping of all God's Laws.

21 v. 22-27. And I saw not temple therein: For the Lord God Almighty and the Lamb are the temple of it.

And the city had no need of the sun, neither the moon, to shine in it: for the glory of God did lighten it, and the Lamb is the light thereof.

And the nations of them which are saved shall walk in the light of it: and the kings of the earth do bring their glory and honour into it.
And the gates of it shall not be shut at all by day: for there shall be no night there.

And they shall bring the glory and honour of the nations into it.

And there shall in no wise enter into it any thing that defileth, neither whatsoever worketh abomination, or maketh a lie: but they which are written in the Lamb's book of life.

The sheer brilliance of this city, illuminated by the presence of God, is awesome, yet all the saved have free access into it and to present the tokens of worship, honour and glory and obedience and be welcomed into that very presence. It seems that the spiritual and material are blended into one.

Chapter 22

22 v. 1-6. And he shewed me a pure river of water of life, clear as crystal, proceeding out of the throne of God and of the Lamb.

In the midst of the street of it, and on either side of the river, was there the tree of life, which bare twelve manner of fruits, and yielded her fruit every month: and the leaves of the tree were for the healing of the nations.

And there shall be no more curse: but the throne of God and of the Lamb shall be in it; and his servants shall serve him:

And they shall see his face; and his name shall be in their foreheads.

And there shall be no night there; and they need no candle, neither light of the sun; for the Lord God giveth them light; and they shall reign forever and ever.

And he said unto me, These saying are faithful and true: And the Lord God of the holy prophets sent his angel to shew unto his servants the things that must shortly be done.

This river is no small stream, and must be of considerable width, as the tree of life grows in it, as well as on either bank. It would seem that the tree has a number of stems, not a remarkable feature as many varieties of tree will strike root and produce new stems where a branch touches the ground, or where a root is exposed to daylight. The healing power of the leaves is however peculiar as there will be no curse there. What we wonder will need that healing? If it ever did there is the cure. There will be no stress disorders caused through working nights!

22 v. 7.   Behold I come quickly: blessed is he that keepeth the sayings of the prophecy of this book.

We are reminded near the end of this vision, as we were at the beginning, that these things are shortly to come to pass. As each section is completed the next is never far away, and we are well advised to watch and be ready for each development. There is again a blessing for taking notice of this vision, no small part of that blessing is to know the purpose of God for this troubled world, and that the Lord Jesus is to return.

22 v. 8-11. And I John saw these things, and heard them. And when I had heard and seen, I fell down to worship before the feet of the angel which shewed me these things.

Then saith he unto me, See thou do it not: for I am thy fellowservant, and of thy brethren the prophets, and of them that keep the sayings of this book: worship God.

And he saith unto me, Seal not the sayings of the prophecy of this book: for the time is at hand.

He that is unjust, let him be unjust still: and he which is filthy, let him be filthy still: and he that is righteous, let him be righteous still: and he that is holy, let him be holy still.

It is hardly surprising after seeing such a vision that John made the mistake of attempting to worship the angel that was his guide and companion. That little incident serves to remind us how easy it is to make mistakes or jump hastily to wrong conclusions, for these things spoken of here are for a time as yet far away from us, even more so for John. *'Seal not... for the time is at hand'*. Shows that we are encouraged to keep the book and our minds open, and take notice of these prophetic visions, and receive blessing and guidance from them. At the very beginning in chapter 1 v. 3, we are exhorted to read, keep and be blessed for reading it, not conditional on our fully understanding every point of it. Strangely, it seems to be rare for the followers of Jesus to take that seriously. At the point when this part of the prophecy is being fulfilled, it seems that there will come a time when there is no further point in the preaching of the gospel for repentance; those who are not already convinced by the amazing revelation of God's glory, are beyond redemption and remain excluded by their own choice and God's mercy from the city and God's presence lest they desecrate the holy place and His indignation should fall upon them. The angels at the gates are there to prevent and protect against such a disaster.

22 v. 12-14. And, behold, I come quickly; and my reward is with me, to give every man according as his work shall be.

I am Alpha and Omega, the beginning and the end, the first and the last.

Blessed are they that do his commandments, that they may have right to the tree of life, and may enter in through the gates into the city.

The vision and prophecy ends here with the signature; I AM. The beginning and the end, will complete His will and purpose, and reminds us whom we serve. We come now to a sort of epilogue.

22 v. 15. For without are dogs, and sorcerers, and whoremongers, and murderers, and idolators, and whosoever loveth and maketh a lie.

The exclusion clause.

22 v.16-17. I Jesus have sent my angel to testify unto you these things in the churches. I am the root and the offspring of David, and the bright and morning star.

And the Spirit and the bride say, Come. And let him that heareth say, Come. And let him that is athirst come. And whosoever will, let him take the water of life freely.

As at the beginning, John was instructed to write to the churches, so at the end Jesus says these things must be proclaimed in the churches! And the Holy Spirit, and the bride, God's servant nation, says come. And all others who are Christ's say come, to take the water of life freely. So we are admonished to continue to evangelise.

22 v. 18-21. For I testify unto every man that heareth the words of the prophecy of this book, If any man shall add unto these things, God shall add unto him the plagues that are written in this book:

And if any man shall take away from the words of the book of this prophecy, God shall take away his part out of the book of life, and out of the holy city, and from the things that are written in this book.

He which testifieth these things saith, Surely I come quickly. Amen. Even so, come, Lord Jesus.

The grace of our Lord Jesus Christ be with you all. Amen.

A stern warning to be true to this word of prophecy.

In this examination of *Revelation*, it has firstly been to look at the actual words given us, this is the most important part, and any comments made are of no value if not supported by *Revelation*, history, other witnesses or the scriptures. It is a task laid upon me by the Lord, and although of limited vision, performed in the hope that those who read, may recognise and align themselves with God's declared purposes, and receive great and wonderful future rewards by His grace and love.

As Moses recorded for us *'... I have set before you life and death, blessing and cursing: therefore choose life, that both thou and thy seed may live'*: (*Deuteronomy* 30 v. 19).

This is presented in the hope that more understanding may result in your greater blessings as promised by the Lord Jesus.

Even so, come, Lord Jesus.

The grace of our Lord Jesus Christ be with you all.